Kid's Guide to Making Money and Keeping It!

Kid's Guide to Making Money and Keeping It!

Judy Bastyra

Illustrations by
Eleanor Taylor

BLOOMSBURY

Published in Great Britain 1997 by
Bloomsbury Children's Books
38 Soho Square, London W1D 5DF

Text copyright © 1997 Judy Bastyra
Illustrations copyright © 1997 Eleanor Taylor

A CIP catalogue record for this book
is available from the British Library

ISBN 0-7475-3271-0
10 9 8 7 6 5 4 3 2 1

Printed and bound in Great Britain
by Clays Ltd, St Ives PLC

For Charles, my inspiration.

Many thanks to my editor,
Helen Wire, for making this book work.

CONTENTS

Chapter One

WHY DO YOU WANT TO MAKE MONEY?

Do you get enough pocket money?
OK, I know the answer already – no. But your parents probably *think* they give you enough or as much as they can afford. This book will show you how to make money for yourself while you are still at school. It will also tell you how to look after your money once you've made it. The *Kid's Guide to Making Money and Keeping It!* is an introduction to the world of commerce – which works on the simple principle of supply and demand.

Once you have decided that you need to supplement your pocket money you will need to know how to do it. As you read on, you will find lots of ideas for how to make lots of dosh out of things you can do or make. Some of them are very simple, while others require certain skills, equipment, and/or money to spend, and they may be better suited to older children. You'll know best which of them you will be able to do. As you try out some of the ideas I hope they will inspire you to think of many more of your own. Who knows, perhaps a few of you will even become multi-millionaires – and all because you learnt how to make a profit out of a good idea while you were still at school.

But first, let's look at some of the many different reasons why young people need more pocket money.

It might be simply to buy sweets, or the latest supersonic video game, a birthday present for your granny, an indestructible Mag-Lite torch, or even a remote-controlled-bubble-gum-blower!

You may need it to pay for your hobbies, such as horse-riding, skating, skate-boarding, tennis, football, model-making, Brownies, Scouts, drama club, music concerts, the cinema, or even eating out with your mates.

Perhaps you could use some extra money to fund your collection of football cards, records, CDs, stamps, stickers, posters, or plastic dinosaurs.

Maybe you're a dedicated follower of fashion. Now, that's an expensive business, whether it's make-up, clothes, or those trainers your mother won't buy you because she thinks they're ugly and you've got six pairs already – totally u n r e a s o n-able!

Or you might want to save up for something that's *really* expensive, like a new 28-speed racing bike that's as light as a feather, a remote controlled boat or car, a state-of-the-art sound system or computer, or even a horse. Maybe you can't wait to leave school and want to save for the happy day when you can take driving lessons, buy your first car or motor bike, take a holiday or flying lessons, travel the world; or, if you're seriously serious, save for your old age!

Whatever it is you need money for, here's a chart to help you work out how much you need to spend each week (expenditure) and therefore how much you will need to earn.

I NEED MONEY:	Weekly Expenditure £
SO I CAN BUY:	
☐	
☐	
☐	
☐	
☐	
☐	
TO PAY FOR MY HOBBIES:	
☐	
☐	
☐	
☐	
☐	
☐	
TO SAVE UP FOR:	
☐	
☐	
☐	
☐	
☐	
☐	
Total I need to earn each week:	£

If it turns out you need to earn a mere £500 per week, you'd better think again. Decide which of the items on your list you *most* want and for which there's at least a chance of you earning enough money. Tick those. The experience you gain by making your own money, now, will all come in useful as you get older and put you well on the way to making your first million.

So, now you have your goal. Buying sweets suddenly doesn't seem so appealing – anyway they're bad for your teeth and you'll only have to save up a lot of money to buy super-white dentures when you're older.

Outside the home, the most common jobs for young teenagers in towns are doing a paper round, helping out in a shop or garden, child-minding, shopping for the elderly or sick, cleaning cars, walking dogs; and in the depths of the country, mucking out the stables, feeding hens, fruit picking (seasonal). Some of the more unusual jobs for children are acting in TV commercials or the theatre, singing, dancing, or photographic modelling for advertisements. Although these glossy jobs can be well paid, there are very strict rules about the hours you can work, your parents or a responsible adult must be with you at all times, and of course you would probably need to be especially attractive and talented.

IMPORTANT WARNING
Before you start on your business career, there are a few things you need to know.

First, you must never put yourself in danger. The best ways of avoiding this are:
- Always tell your parents what you are doing, where you are going, and what time you expect to be home.
- Try to work for people you and your parents both know and trust.
- Never go alone into a stranger's house or car.
- Try to work as a team with a friend.

- Don't take on jobs that require using poisonous substances or where there are toxic fumes.

Second, you mustn't let your business activities interfere with your school work. In fact, in the United Kingdom, if you are employed by another person you are *legally* only allowed to work a certain number of hours while you are under the minimum school leaving age, which is 16.

UNDER 10
Full-time employment not allowed.

10–12-YEAR-OLDS: Anytime: 2 hours per day
Current bylaws allów the employment by parents or guardians of 10–12-year-olds to do some light agricultural or horticultural work. That is, you can be paid to do jobs such as feeding the hens and raking up autumn leaves, but only one of the hours can be worked *before* school.

13–14-YEAR-OLDS
Schooldays: 2 hours per day
Only one of the work hours can be before school.
Weekend: total work hours must not exceed 7.
Saturdays: 5 hours maximum
Sundays: 2 hours (change to 4 hours proposed)
It is proposed to raise the number of hours a child can be employed on a Sunday to a maximum of 4 hours but these must be worked between 7–11 a.m.
School Holidays: 5 hours per day (maximum of 25 hours per week).

15–16-YEAR-OLDS
Schooldays: 2 hours per day
Only one hour worked can be before school.
Weekend: total work hours not to exceed 10
Saturday: 8 hours maximum
Sunday: 2 hours maximum (between 7–11 a.m.)

13

It is proposed to raise the maximum time you can be employed on a Sunday to 8 hours but over the whole weekend you should not work more than 10 hours.

School Holidays: 8 hours per day (maximum of 35 hours per week).

The above is for general guidance only. There are also very strict licensing laws regarding how much time children can work in entertainment industries, such as acting, singing and dancing in films, theatres, or circuses. For definitive information, your parents or proposed employer should phone the local borough council or HMSO (Her Majesty's Stationery Office) to check the current bylaws.

Chapter Two

WHAT ARE YOU GOOD AT?

The easiest way to be good at something is to enjoy what you are doing. So, first let's identify what you like to do, what you are good at, and what you can't bear; then we can look at how you might make some money. Tick the box next to anything that applies to you in the following lists.

I REALLY ENJOY:

- [ ] computer graphics
- [ ] computer games
- [x] inventing
- [x] making things
- [x] cooking
- [x] woodwork
- [ ] metalwork
- [ ] mechanics
- [ ] sewing
- [x] knitting
- [x] photography
- [x] reading
- [x] drawing
- [ ] writing: stories, letters, poetry
- [x] making up jokes
- [x] making people laugh
- [ ] pleasing people
- [ ] old people
- [ ] babies
- [x] animals
- [ ] being alone

- [x] being with people
- [ ] helping people
- [ ] looking after people
- [x] being indoors
- [x] being outdoors
- [ ] physical activities (I'm strong)
- [ ] acting, dancing, singing, gymnastics
- [ ] playing musical instrument
- [x] gardening
- [ ] sport
- [x] collecting things
- [x] buying and/or selling things
- [ ] pop music
- [x] cinema
- [ ] fashion
- [ ] washing up, housework
- [ ] caring for the environment
- [x] shopping
- [ ] other

I AM GOOD AT:

- ☐ being tidy
- ☑ being creative
- ☐ being energetic
- ☑ talking to anyone
- ☐ playing with little kids
- ☐ being patient
- ☑ mathematics
- ☐ saving money
- ☐ spending money
- ☐ being sensible and responsible

- ☐ looking after my little brothers and sisters
- ☐ changing nappies
- ☑ first aid
- ☐ cycling
- ☑ swimming, life saving
- ☑ playing piano or other instrument
- ☑ writing song lyrics
- ☑ writing poetry

I DON'T LIKE:

- ☐ using the phone
- ☐ talking to people
- ☐ working with people
- ☑ adults who make me nervous
- ☑ waiting (I'm impatient)
- ☑ babies and little kids
- ☐ changing nappies

- ☐ hard work (I'm too weak)
- ☑ bad smells (make me puke)
- ☐ housework of any kind
- ☐ outdoor activities
- ☑ saving money
- ☑ other

Now you have worked out what sort of person you are and what you like doing, you should be able to decide the kind of work to which you are most suited. Although you can probably think of lots more, here are a few suggestions:

OUTDOORS/SPORTY TYPE

Gardening: You should be quite strong. Plant bulbs; rake leaves; weeding; lawn mowing.

Dog walking: You must like dogs and be able to keep them under control.

Coaching sport: You must like younger children and know the rules of your game.

Teaching young children to cycle: You must be strong, be able to cycle yourself, and probably know some first-aid!

Lifeguard at a swimming party: You must have a life-saving certificate.

Entertainment: You must be able to juggle, have football skills, play a musical instrument, or put on a play.

Paper round: You must be able to get up early. A bike would speed up the delivery time and carry the weight of the newspapers.

Car cleaning: Start with cars belonging to trusted friends and relatives. You may see children cleaning windscreens at traffic lights for small tips, but *don't ever do this*. It is illegal and very dangerous. Also you would be inhaling a lot of toxic fumes that damage your lungs and brain!

Pets: Cleaning out cages; washing the dog; emptying the litter tray (who wouldn't willingly pay someone to do this?); holiday care.

Rubbish: Take it out weekly (just before the bin men come) and clean up afterwards.

Farm Work: Muck out stables, hen houses, etc.; sell manure to gardeners.

Bicycle repairs: Offer to repair punctures, clean and oil; customize bikes by painting them with personalized designs

INDOORS/STUDIOUS TYPE

Shop: Shop for people; or work in a shop.

Teach: Music; a foreign language/conversation; homework; any skill you have.

Housework: Cleaning, ironing, washing-up, window cleaning (ground floor only!); silver polishing.

Catering: Waiting on tables; washing-up; party services; cooking to sell.

Drawing and Painting: Customize Nintendos, Gameboys, or bikes by painting a unique design for their owners; draw or paint pet portraits.

Entertainment: At children's parties: puppeteer, clown, face-painting, funky nail-painter, juggler, hair-braiding, magician.

Fashion: Set a trend by making zany clothes or jewellery and selling them to friends.

Recycling: Make brilliant things out of old clothes, drink cans, paper, etc. and sell them. Sell your old toys, books, comics, etc.

Collecting: Sell collections you've become bored by, or look for things that other collectors want to buy; buy and sell at car-boot fairs.

Baby-sitting: Playing with or reading to young children. You will need an adult close by to help in case of accident or emergency.

Writing: Enter stories or poems for competitions; write an essay about an issue you feel strongly about and send it to a magazine that you like to read. Or write to the letters page of newspapers and magazines. Many of them offer £5-10 for the best letter of the week.

Making Things to Sell: Paint portraits of people and/or pets; friendship bracelets; *papier-mâché* bowls, ornaments, etc.; pomanders; picture frames; toys for pets; doll's house furniture; puppets; bean bags for babies; notepaper; paint or print pictures on T-shirts, etc.

Adult Parties: Cloakroom attendant; waiter; help prepare for, and clean up afterwards.

Rising Stars: Photographic model; actor; film extra; performance artist; musician. But there are strict licensing laws regarding children working in entertainment. Ring your local borough council or Her Majesty's Stationery Office (phone: 0171 873 0011) to check what the current regulations are.

Fund-raiser: Organize parties; seek sponsorship and run sponsored events for charities.

To help you work out what you can do to earn money, fill in the following chart from the above lists as well as adding other ideas of your own. Compare what you enjoy doing (column A) with what you're good at (column B) then you should be able to work out in columns C and D what jobs you will be good at doing.

A. WHAT I ENJOY MOST	B. WHAT I'M GOOD AT	C. SUITABLE INDOOR JOBS	D. SUITABLE OUTDOOR JOBS

The Budget

To make sure you have plenty of time for the fun things you want to do, you won't want to work for a moment longer than you have to in order to earn the money you need. To manage this, you are going to have to know how to work out a *budget*. All businesses do a yearly budget so they can predict what they will have to earn to cover their expenses *and* make a profit. If you only have a certain amount of money to spend each week, working out a budget will also help you to sort out how to manage your money and not spend more than you have. And it will tell you how much extra you will have to earn if you want to be able to spend more.

Budgeting is a good way to begin to understand how money works. It may sound deadly dull, *but,* as much as we'd all like to live like kings (money no object), budgeting is an essential part of life for most people.

How to Work Out a Budget

Write down everything you have to spend money on, whether it's bus fares, lunch money, going out, or buying CDs, sweets or snacks. Deduct the amount of pocket money you get, and you will then know how much extra you have to earn.

Here's a sample budget:

Expenses per Week

Bus fares	£ 4.00
Lunches	£10.00
Club	£ 2.00
Saving for special clothes, shoes, bike, presents, etc.	£ 7.00
Total weekly expenses	£23.00
Less contribution from parents	£20.00
Minimum amount I need to earn	**£ 3.00**

In chapters five to nine there are instructions for how to make things; what it will cost you; and how to go about providing services and getting work. But, before you start having the fun of doing that, you are going to need to know how to market your goods or services. That is, you are going to need some business nous!

Chapter Three

HOW TO MAKE MONEY

Research, Planning, Organization and Negotiating Skills

Research and Planning

When you want to start a business, research and planning are vital. The aim of all business is to make a profit, that is to make more money than it costs to run the business. If you are thinking of providing a service or making goods to sell, you first need to answer some questions:

- How much will it cost to set up?
- What equipment do I need? Can I borrow it?
- How long does it take to do?
- How much do I want to earn?
- Where are my potential customers/clients?
- Would they be willing to pay me what I would have to charge in order to make a profit?
- How can I advertise my goods or services?
- What is the competition?
- How can I provide a better deal than my competitors?
- Will it be possible to expand in the future?

Time spent planning and researching will help you to avoid making expensive mistakes and will also give you more of a chance to make your business a success.

With your parents' permission, of course, make good use of the telephone (you may need to pay them 10p per call). You will find a lot of useful information in the *Yellow Pages* about your competitors, or where to get things you need, or who you might approach locally for work. It will save you walking all over town and wasting a lot of time when you need to know something. It's also a good way to check if shops or other people might be interested in buying what you've made or possibly using your services.

Here is an example of how you might go about setting up a carwash business. You can apply the same method to any business, whether it be making or dealing in things to sell, or providing a service.

CHARLIE'S CARWASH

Research and Planning

1. Seek Advice
Ask your parents to show you how to clean a car really well. Then try bartering a service in return for goods. Suggest that if they provide you with the basic equipment you will wash their car twice for free. You will then have the tools of your trade at no (monetary) cost to you.

2. Check out the Competition
Read the noticeboards in newsagents and supermarkets. Look at advertising in the local newspapers and leaflets that come through the letterbox. Perhaps your mother could phone up to check the prices of what is on offer. Go to the local carwash and check out the costs for the various services. To be attractive, your service is going to

have to cost less and be more convenient for the customer or client.

3. Time Yourself

Do a trial clean on your family car, which should be good and dirty before you start. Remember, this will count as one of the free cleans you've promised your parents. Make yourself a chart and note down the time it takes for the various stages. Get ready, go . . .

SERVICE STAGES	TIME TAKEN
Wash	31 minutes.
Rinse and dry	21
Wax and Polish	47
Chromework (on classic cars)	40
Valeting (clean inside)	30
Pack up	5
Total	174 minutes (nearly 3 hours!)

Another element of time you shouldn't forget is how long it takes you to get to and from the job. If it takes 10 minutes then you should include a charge for this time in your costing. Try to get jobs within 10–15 minutes from home.

4. Expenses (Cost of Equipment and Materials)

The cost of your materials (including a small amount for wear and tear on your equipment) is an important part of your costing. For example:

EQUIPMENT	INITIAL OUTLAY	COST PER JOB
Car wash detergent	£2.00 (6 washes)	£0.33
Wax/Polish	£2.50 (2 waxes)	£1.25
Chamois-type cloth	£0.99 (20 washes)	£0.05
Sponge	£0.99 (20 washes)	£0.05
Bucket	£2.50 (50 washes)	£0.05
Total initial outlay:	**£8.98**	
	Total cost per job:	**£1.73**

Cut your costs as much as you can by borrowing equipment or making use of things that your family has finished with, such as old clothes or towels, bathroom sponges (don't use scratchy ones on car paintwork though), etc.

5. Working Out Your Price

If want to make £3.00 per hour (5p per minute) you can now work out your prices. This is how Charlie worked out his carwash charges (including the 15p for wear and tear on his equipment). It is based on the figures in sections *3. Time Yourself* (page 25) and *4. Expenses* (above).

SERVICE	TIME COST (£3 per hour)	MATERIALS	TRAVEL	TOTAL CHARGE
REGULAR Wash, rinse, dry	£1.80	£0.48	nil	£2.28
ONE STAR Wash, rinse, dry, wax and polish	£5.20	£1.73	nil	£6.93
GOLD STAR Wash, rinse, dry, wax, polish and chromework	£7.20	£1.73	nil	£8.93
DE LUXE Wash, rinse, dry, wax, polish, chromework plus full valeting (cleaning inside)	£8.70	£1.73	nil	£10.43

For similar services in a professional carwash, the charges range from £4–6 for a simple wash to £15 for a complete (de luxe) service including silicone waxing and tire dressing. This means it would be cheaper for a client to use Charlie's Carwash (even if he rounded up his charges to the nearest 50p). As long as he cleans the car as well as, or better than, the professional carwash Charlie will have earned himself a regular client and will have more money in his pocket than he would have had he slumped in front of the telly all afternoon.

Whatever your business enterprise, always compare your charges with your competitor's prices. If they are about the same you may want to reduce yours slightly. Don't forget that as you become more experienced you will get faster and more cost effective. That is, you'll use up *less* of your time to earn the same amount of money.

Once you've worked out your costing, the next thing to do is to get organized and go out and find your market (customers/clients).

ORGANIZATION AND NEGOTIATION

You will need to keep an appointment diary and make a list of the services you are offering. Be sure to stress what a *superior hand-finished service* you are offering. For example, Charlie could claim his carwash was *great value for money* and there'd be *no need to drive to the carwash*.

The cheapest way of getting customers is to talk to friends and neighbours. At the weekend, offer your skills to your neighbours. If you are selling something, take a sample of what you have made, or if you're offering car washing, make sure the family car is always pristine. Your potential clients can then inspect your work. It will be your best reference.

When you are taking bookings for your services try to be a little flexible. It may be raining on the Saturday morning you've arranged but you won't want to lose the

27

	Saturday	Sunday	Monday	Tuesday	Wed'day	Thursday	Friday
7.00 a.m.							
8.00							
9.00							
10.00							
11.00							
12.00 p.m							
1.00							
2.00							
3.00							
4.00							
5.00							
6.00 +							

work. So keep a note of any alternative times convenient to each client; and *always* ring them make a new date *as soon as you know you can't keep an appointment*. Adults don't like waiting around for someone who doesn't turn up. Remember, a cross customer is a lost customer.

So that you never miss an appointment and can keep track of all your responsibilities, it would be a good idea to draw up a weekly timetable for yourself. You could enlarge the basic planner on page 26 by photocopying it. Fill in all the fun things you want to do for yourself first. Next, put an X across all the regular times you spend at school, and doing such things as playing sport, or music lessons. That will make it very easy to spot where you have time free for other projects.

NEGOTIATION

You may have to do some negotiating. Most people love to get a bargain. It feels good to knock down the price of something you want to buy. You could start with your prices a little higher than they need to be and then *reluctantly* lower them. Or you could offer a discount for a multiple booking, say 10% off on a booking for eight washes. Or you could offer a loyalty bonus. Give your customer a voucher after every wash. When they have eight vouchers, offer them a regular wash, free.

FUTURE PLANNING

When your business has been running for a while, you need to step back and have a look at it in an analytical way.

What problems have you encountered?

For example, if you've washed cars over three weekends you may have discovered:

- Much bigger cars take longer to clean.
- The people at No. 16 have three long-haired dogs and their car is always full of dog hair and mud.

- One Sunday you had to clean 12 cars because the weather had been so bad on the Saturday.
- However well and carefully you clean the car at No. 5 the customer always complains and won't pay the full amount.

You need to find solutions to any problems you encounter. You could introduce a special tariff for big estate vehicles or *doggy* cars. Give up cleaning the car at No. 5. And if you find yourself with too many cars to wash in one day, you could employ some of your friends.

You could also ask them to help you expand your business to the next street.

EXPANDING YOUR BUSINESS

If you employ your friends you will increase your turnover, which is the amount of money you earn before you deduct your expenses. You can pay your friends £2.00 per hour while still charging your customers on the basis of £3.00 per hour. This means you will earn £1.00 for the time and effort you put into organizing the work without actually having to do it.

If you are going to trust your valued customers to your friends, then you will have to:
- train them to work to the same high standards that you do.
- supply them with a set of tools for the job.
- check that they arrive on time for all jobs and then do the work properly.

At the same time, you will always be looking for new customers.

Remember: When you are providing a regular service, your customers will rely on you. So, for example, if you are going on holiday, make sure that you let them know *beforehand*; or organize a reliable friend to cover for you. If your customers can't depend on you, you will soon lose their business.

Planning and researching a business is always valuable because it will save your business money. However, no matter how well organized you think you are, something unexpected is always likely to crop up. So, be flexible and adapt quickly to deal with any problems that arise. Remember, there is always more than one way to do anything.

Now, go out and get those customers!

NO CASH? THEN TRY BARTERING

Bartering is another form of negotiating the sale of goods or services. It is a way of *buying and selling* without any money changing hands. You can trade goods or services for something you want that is of a similar value. It's a bit like swapping.

For example, you can barter a service in exchange for another service. If your sister wants her hamster's cage cleaned out, you can offer to do it for her if she takes two of your turns at the washing-up. Or, your elder brother might help you with your homework in exchange for you cleaning his football boots or tidying his room. Use all your best negotiating skills to make sure any slight inequality in the worth of the services is in your favour!

You can exchange goods of equal worth. Your friend may make brilliant friendship bracelets and you don't have any money to buy one. But if you were a good cook, you could exchange a bag of home-made fudge for a bracelet.

In some ways, bartering makes a lot more sense than money because money is really only pieces of paper and bits of metal. Afterall, would you rather be washed up alone on a desert island with a £100 note or a packet of chocolate biscuits?

JOBS ON CREDIT

If your family do a lot of job swapping but don't always have enough cash to pay for them immediately, you can organize a credit system. Keep a book in which you note down the value of each job you do for one another. Then at the end of the week or month (preferably just after you all receive your pocket money) you can work out how much actual money has to be paid over. The one who does most work will, of course, never have to pay out any money. If you all compete hard for this, you could have the most efficiently run household in the country!

Chapter Four

PROMOTING YOUR BUSINESS

Networking, Advertising, Marketing, and Customer Relations

NETWORKING

Who You Know

Have you heard the expression, 'it's not *what* you know but *who you know*'? Well, it's not always true but *who you know* can sometimes help – especially if you know someone who works successfully in the kind of business that you want to set up.

You know how boring it is when your parents want to show you off at their parties and you have to stand around looking politely interested even after 26 people have told

you you're the spitting image of your mad uncle Bert? Well, next time, don't be too hasty. Think, *Is there any way I can make a profit out of this situation?* In return for some service, your parents may be willing to pay you for the privilege of having you there! You could hand round the peanuts, pour drinks, or act as cloakroom attendant (that is, take the visitor's coats when they arrive). You could even offer to clear up after the party (for a slightly higher fee of course). Your parents could then relax and go straight to bed at the end of the evening knowing they wouldn't have to wake up to the horrible debris of foul ashtrays, smelly wine glasses, and plates covered in left-over curry and rice or stale chocolate cake (Yuk!).

Encourage your parents to party over the weekend as they probably won't let you stay up late if there's school in the morning. They might even give you extra money for hoovering the room as well.

Always look at any adult gathering from the view point of **networking**. It might be a bit yawn-making when great Uncle· Harry tells you yet again about his 50 years as a senior manager in the Post Office; or Aunt Kate imagines you're utterly fascinated by the swinging sixties when she worked in the music business, wore a mini-skirt, multi-coloured eye shadow, and white plastic boots, and danced all night to soul music.

Don't knock it! If you are interested in collecting (see page 72), old Uncle Harry just might happen to know loads of collectors and dealers. And Aunt Kate is bound to have some really cool old records and is likely to know loads of people in the business who have the power to hire and fire today's disc jockeys! She may not have a record player any more and have no use for her old records. She might even be prepared to lend or give them to you to help you in your new business as a . . . disc jockey. She may want to get rid of her old clothes that no longer fit her. Combining two of your interests, you might organize a sixties party and hire out the clothes; or since they are now back in fashion, you could sell them.

ALWAYS REMEMBER TO:

Ask Questions and Listen: Grown-ups are flattered to be asked for advice. Encourage them to give you information by asking them questions. Listen to everything they have to say before you offer your own opinion. If you interrupt them in full flow you might miss a piece of information that could be vital to your future success.

Keep a Notebook: Jot down any problems or questions you need advice about for your new business venture. Carry it with you always so you're prepared whenever you meet an adult who could help you. You don't want to forget to ask a vital question when you get the opportunity.

Write Thank-you Notes: Always write a note of thanks when an adult has given you a present or been especially helpful. Make it entertaining (not just a dull *duty* letter) by adding drawings or relevant jokes, and tell them about your business plans. If you let them feel involved they'll be happy to help you again and may even come up with some good ideas for you.

Be Polite: When dealing with customers, always be polite and helpful. Remember *the customer is always right* – especially when they are paying you loads of money.

A good telephone manner is essential to a successful business. Make a real effort to sound friendly and helpful on the phone. Speak very clearly and introduce yourself. If you're making a call, say: *Good morning/afternoon, my name is —, I'm calling to ask —etc.* If you are answering the phone, give the name of your business and ask, *How may I help you?*

Networking is also very important when you are promoting your business. If you intend to send out leaflets to advertise your services or to sell your products, it's good to start with people you know. You can then ask them for names of some of their friends who may be interested in what you have to offer. That way you can build up a list of interested contacts to whom you can *target* your advertising, marketing and promotions. This will save you money. For example, if your leaflet (that cost you 4p to produce) is offering bicycle repairs, it would be wasted on a 95-year-old pensioner who never leaves the house!

ADVERTISING AND MARKETING

Advertising and marketing are what you do to let people know you have something to sell or have a service to offer, and persuading them that they want it. The cheapest way to advertise is by *word-of-mouth*, that is done by people who you've worked for recommending you to their friends.

Other ways are flyers (leaflets), posters, newspaper advertisements, and newsagents' noticeboards. Knocking on doors can't really be recommended (unless you know all your neighbours) as, nowadays, people have become very wary of strangers who come to the door. And it might be risky for you too.

Flyers are one of the best ways to tell potential customers *everything* about your product or service. Unless you're prepared to sit down and write (neatly!) the same information a hundred times, the easiest way to produce a leaflet is by having access to a computer and printer. If you do have to handwrite/draw it, maybe you know someone who would be willing to photocopy it free for you. Or, perhaps the local print shop could be talked into reducing their rates or printing your leaflet free in return for some service you could offer them. For example, you could offer to deliver advertising leaflets for them.

Advertising in local newspapers can be costly. The classified *For Sale* columns are usually the cheapest way to advertise and some papers print these small ads free. Better still, if you can make your business enterprise sound as if it would be of interest to readers, a newspaper editor might be persuaded to have an article written about you to be printed in the features, or junior section of the paper. You wouldn't have to pay for this but lots of people would read about you and your business. Contact your local paper, tell them what you're doing, and include a sample of something you've made and/or a photograph of you at work that they could print.

How to Write and Design a Flyer

To make people read it, your flyer must be eye-catching. It must clearly tell your potential customers all about your business and how to contact you. Make it easy for them. Here's a checklist of what to include:

- Eye-catching border and headline.
- Information about the business.
- Rates or prices.
- Availability (weekends only/after 4 p.m./etc.)
- References.
- Your name, address and phone number.

If you've had experience walking your own dog, you might advertise your services as a dog walker with a flyer like the one on page 38.

TOO BUSY TO

WALK THE DOG?

RESPONSIBLE DOG WALKER

8 years experience!
Also available:
Cat-litter tray emptying

Available:
Weekends (all day)
Monday-Friday after 4 p.m.

Competitive Rates:
£2.00 per hour, per dog
50p per cat-litter tray

Dave's Pet Care

Telephone: 142 1842
between 5.30 and 7.30

☆☆☆☆☆☆☆ **REFERENCES AVAILABLE** ☆☆☆☆☆☆☆

Chapter Five

MAKING THINGS TO SELL
Cooking, Making, Sewing, Modelling

If you are the kind of person who enjoys making things, this chapter will give you ideas and instructions for some easy things to cook, or make to sell. For these projects you may need to invest some money to buy materials, ingredients, tools or utensils. But before you spend any money, always ask your parents if they will lend you their tools or even provide the ingredients. They might be pleased to see you making an effort to earn extra pocket money! If you want to be really businesslike, you could repay them by offering them 5% of your profits!

COOKING TO SELL

Advertising and Marketing: Distribute flyers *before* you go into production. That way you need only cook enough to fulfil your orders, you won't have wasted any ingredients on unsold goods, and your produce will always be fresh (a major selling point!). To win your first customers you may have to cook a batch and give away free bite-size samples. If they're delicious, you're bound to get some orders. Wrap each in a twist of cellophane and add a small label giving the price, your business name and phone number, and state, **For orders: please give 48 hours notice.**

Distribute flyers locally, put up posters in clubs, school, church or village halls, libraries, supermarket and news-agents' windows, etc. Give away samples of your cooking at school together with a flyer.

Presentation and Packaging

One of the secrets of selling anything you make is good presentation. If it looks nice people will buy it. So, what-ever you are selling, remember it is worth making an effort to package it wonderfully. Whenever you are given something in a pretty box, don't chuck it, keep it. You never know when it will come in useful.

If you don't happen to have any boxes handy, you can always make your own. Take a ready-made carton (like a tea-bag box) to pieces and you will see that it is very cleverly constructed from one piece of cardboard. Work out from that how to make boxes of the size you need. When you're adding up how much time you spend making something to sell, don't forget to include the time it takes to package or wrap your goods.

But first, you'll need something to sell.

HOW THE COOKIE CRUMBLES

At last! Now you know how to market your product you can get on with what you enjoy doing – some delicious cooking. There are a few recipes in this book to get you started. As you become a proficient cook you will be able to adjust and invent recipes to suit your own taste and the quantities required to fulfil your orders. Start looking through other books and magazines to find more recipes you could make and sell successfully. For example, you could bake and decorate birthday cakes to order – draw pictures of your designs on your advertising flyer.

Special Equipment and Packaging

Before embarking on a baking career, you (or your parents) will need to have these utensils:

Weighing scales	*Silver foil*
Mixing bowl	*Baking tin or foil tray*
Electric mixer	*Paper patty cases*
Spoons	*Wire cooling rack*
Palette knife	*A cooker!*

Cake boxes: Ask at a local cake shop where they buy their cake boxes; make your own; or recycle used packaging (again empty dry-food boxes can easily be turned inside-out and decorated).

Take my Advice!
Don't start cooking or baking 10 minutes
before supper has to be prepared.

Always take care when handling hot dishes or electrical equipment and only use a hot oven when there is a responsible adult in the house.

The measures given in the recipes are metric with

imperial equivalents in brackets. Use one or the other, not a combination of the two. If you make double the amounts given, you will increase your profit margin because you will have twice as many cakes to sell, but it won't have cost you any extra time.

Brownies

Brownies must be one of the all-time favourite chocolate treats. You can make them to sell individually or bake them on disposable foil trays and sell them by the trayful.

Makes: 16 brownies
Time: 30 minutes, plus cooling time
Approximate cost: £3 for 16 (19p each)
Selling price: 35p each (x 16 = £5.60)
Profit: £2.60

Ingredients

125 g (5 oz) plain chocolate
100 g (4 oz) butter
5 eggs
400 g (14 oz) sugar

1 tsp vanilla essence
100 g (4 oz) plain flour
50 g (2 oz) cocoa powder
¼ tsp salt

1. Heat the oven to 190°C (375°F) or gas mark 5. Line a baking tray with silver foil and lightly butter it.
2. Melt the chocolate and butter together in a double-boiler, or in a heat-proof bowl in a microwave (600W) for two minutes on medium. Set aside to cool.
3. Beat the eggs until frothy. Add and mix in the sugar and vanilla essence. Stir this into the cooled chocolate.
4. Gently fold the flour, cocoa and salt into the chocolate mixture. Spread evenly over the baking tray and bake for 20 minutes.
5. Wear oven gloves to remove from the oven. While still warm, cut into 16 squares or other shapes if you have some biscuit-cutters.

Shopping Tip: Brownies are expensive to make because you use only the best ingredients. If you can buy in bulk, ingredients tend to be cheaper. Look for special offers at the supermarket.

Business Tip: To justify the price you want to charge, brownies must be marketed as a *luxury* item. Make them irresistible by packaging them to look as good as possible. For example, a good name might be *Super Scrumptious Chocolate Brownie*s.

Fairy Cakes

Fairy cakes are a doddle to make and you can decorate them in many amusing ways.

Makes: 16 fairy cakes
Time: 30 minutes, plus cooling time
Approximate cost: cakes £2.56 for 16 (16p each)
Selling price: 25p each (x 16 = £4.00)
Profit: £1.44

Ingredients for Cakes
100 g (4 oz) butter or
  margarine
100 g (4 oz) sugar
2 eggs, beaten
100 g (4 oz) self-raising flour
1 tsp vanilla essence

Flavouring (one only):
1 tsp grated lemon zest
2 tbls cocoa powder
1 tsp grated orange zest
For the Glacé Icing:
100 g (4 oz) icing sugar
2 tbls water
Sweets for decoration

1. Heat the oven to 180°C (350°F) or gas mark 4. Line two eight-cup patty tins with paper cases.
2. In a mixing bowl, cream together the butter (or

margarine) and sugar until light and fluffy.

3. Add and mix in the beaten eggs and the flour, a little of each at a time. Add and mix in your chosen flavouring. Spoon the mixture into the paper cases.
4. Bake for about 15 minutes. Wear oven gloves to remove the tins from the oven. Set aside to cool.
5. When cool, decorate the cakes with glacé icing and sweets.

Decorating Fairy Cakes
The glacé icing can be coloured with drops of food colouring. Press dried fruits or little sweets into the icing to make pirate, clown, cat, or teddybear faces, or pictures of flowers and other patterns.

Shopping Tip: See *Brownies* tip (page 41).

Business Tip: Fairy cakes are always popular. Apart from selling the cakes to be eaten at a party, you could provide a party invitation service. A novel idea would be to write the invitation round small paper plates and hand them out with a fairy cake on each.

You'd need to think of a clever way of transporting them without damage. You could gather cellophane up over the cake, tie a ribbon round it, add a name label, then dangle the plates on different lengths of ribbon or thread from an old broomstick. Place the broomstick over your shoulder and deliver the invitations.

These invitations would be great fun to do and deliver but would take a long time to make. Your potential customers may think they were too expensive if you costed in your time realistically. But, you might think it worth doing anyway for the pleasure of hearing everyone tell you how brilliant you are! At least try to charge a bit more than it cost you to buy materials.

You can also try and invent other exciting and unusual ways of making party invitations.

SWEETS

Sweets are always easy to sell. The profit is usually quite high (as long as *you* don't eat too many of them as you cook). Most people who aren't too sensible *love* sweets.

Try making the following two recipes for fudge and truffles. Once you have sold them successfully you can increase your range by making other kinds of sweets. Look for other recipes for sweets such as peppermint creams, coconut ice; fruit shapes moulded out of marzipan. Decorate them with nuts, or roll them in desiccated coconut or chocolate sprinkles.

Fudge

Fudge is an excellent sweet to sell because it's simple to make and everyone loves it – from tiny children to grown-ups. You can vary the basic recipe by adding different flavourings. Wrap them in see-through cellophane or pop them in paper *petit four* cases. Always present them attractively and then you will be able to charge a lot for HAND-MADE LUXURY CANDIES.

Makes: Approximately 50 pieces
Time: 30 minutes, plus cooling time
Approximate cost: £1.25
Selling price: £2.50 (5p per cube. 50p for 10)
Profit: £1.25

Ingredients
Oil for greasing the tin
450 g (1 lb) caster sugar
75 g (3 oz) butter
150 ml (5 fl oz) milk
175 ml (6 fl oz) evaporated
  milk

½ tsp vanilla essence
100 g (4 oz) sultanas
1 tbl rum essence or
  3 tbls rum

Take my Advice!
Boiling sugar is very DANGEROUS.
Ask an adult to help you.

---

1. Lightly oil a shallow 18 cm (7 in) square baking tray. Put the sugar, butter, milk and evaporated milk into a saucepan and place over a gentle heat. Cook for a few minutes, stirring constantly until the sugar is dissolved.
2. Turn up the heat a little and bring to the boil without stirring. Reduce the heat to bring it to a steady boil. Cook for about 30 minutes, stirring from time to time. To test if it is cooked enough, drop a tiny bit into a bowl of cold water. It should form a soft ball.
3. Remove the pan from the heat and stir in the vanilla essence, sultanas, and rum essence (or rum). Beat the mixture vigorously with a wooden spoon until it becomes grainy and thick.
4. Pour the mixture into the tin and score the surface into 50 squares. Leave to cool and set completely before cutting it up into squares. Store in airtight container.

Advertising and Marketing: The best way to advertise fudge is to eat it in front of other people, smacking your lips ecstatically. Then offer them a piece and, hey presto, they will place an order! If that doesn't work, try flyers and posters or set up a stall in your front garden if there are enough passers-by where you live.

Presentation: Little boxes, baskets or cellophane bags, ribbon. It is important to wrap the fudge attractively either in see-through paper like cellophane or in a box. Always put a sticker on it with your phone number, and enclose an order form.

Truffles

Chocolate truffles are most adults' favourite sweets. They think they're sophisticated and like to serve them with coffee at dinner parties. So, the whole image of the truffle is mega EXPENSIVE!

Makes: about 20 truffles
Time: $1\frac{1}{2}$ hours
Approx. cost to make: £2.00 (10p per truffle)
Selling price: £1.00 for a packet of 5 (x 4 = £4.00)
Profit: £2.00

Ingredients
6–12 tbls unsalted butter
350 g (12 oz) best quality
 plain chocolate

Coating:
75 g (3 oz) plain chocolate,
 grated
$1\frac{1}{2}$ tbls cocoa powder

1. Melt the butter in a small saucepan over a low heat. Add the chocolate and cook, stirring constantly until it is completely melted.
2. Remove from the heat and allow to cool slightly before chilling in the fridge for 1 hour.

3. Meanwhile, line a baking sheet with wax paper. Remove the truffle mixture from the fridge and scoop out tea-spoonfuls on to the baking sheet.
4. Sprinkle the grated chocolate into a shallow bowl and the cocoa powder into another one.
5. Your hands should be cold and dry as you form each teaspoonful into a ball. Roll each one in the cocoa powder, then in the grated chocolate.
6. Store in a paper box in the fridge.

Advertising and Marketing: Networking is the best way to market truffles. Give your granny or aunt and uncle some as a present to serve at a dinner party. They could take orders for you. Truffles sell very well at fêtes but the profits will go to charity. However, you could include an advertising flyer in every packet of truffles you donate. Give a truffle to all the neighbours you *know*, and expand your market by visiting with your friends the neighbours who *they know* near where they live. They'll soon be hooked if you give them one to try, free.

PARTY SAVOURIES

Lots of people prefer to eat savoury food at parties and would gladly pay you to provide some imaginative snacks for them. You could organize the food for a children's party with a jungle theme. Use pizza dough to make delicious hot food in the shape of all kinds of animals, such as:

Pizza Snakes

Makes: 2 snakes (enough for 10 kids)
Time: At least 1½ hours
Approx. cost to make: £3.00
Selling price: £6 for 2 snakes
Profit: £3.00

Ingredients
Pizza Dough:
300 g (10 oz) plain flour,
Sprinkle of flour (for
  kneading/rolling out)
½ tsp salt
15 g (1 sachet) easy-blend
  dried yeast
2 tbls olive oil
1 tsp olive oil to grease the
  bowl
250 ml (9 fl oz) hot water

Topping:
Ready-made tomato sauce
Ground black pepper
250 g (8 oz) Mozzarella
  cheese, square slices
Black olives

Optional extras:
Mixed herbs, oregano, basil,
onion, garlic, mushrooms,
peppers, sweetcorn,
pineapple chunks.

1. Sift the flour and salt into a large mixing bowl.
2. Add the yeast, oil and hot water and mix into a dough. Form it into a ball.
3. Sprinkle some flour on to your work surface then knead the dough on it for five minutes.
4. Oil a clean bowl and put the dough into it. Cover with some cling film or a clean tea towel and leave to rise for one hour in a dry place.
5. Heat the oven to 190°C (375°F) or gas mark 5. Oil two baking trays. Halve the dough and roll out each half into a snake.
6. Place each snake on a baking sheet. Spoon the tomato sauce over it (including any of the optional extras). Arrange squares of cheese in diagonal pattern along the snake's back. Bake in the oven for 15–20 minutes.

7. Wear oven gloves to take it out of the oven. Press chopped olives into the hot, softened cheese to make a pattern and the snake's eyes.

Cook's Tip: Whenever you have any spare time, make some dough and freeze it. Your pizza will then only take you about 30 minutes to make.

Revolting Rolls

These make the perfect football supporters! They're great to serve at a football party. Take your favourite bread rolls, fill them with sandwich fillings of your choice. Then create crazy faces on the top of them by fixing bits of fruit and vegetable with cocktail sticks. Use such things as cress for hair (attach by making shallow incisions in the roll); cucumber, radishes, olives, carrots, etc, for eyes. For a grinning mouth insert slices of cheese for teeth. Use the cocktail sticks to pick off the features and pop them into your mouth without taking your eyes off the goal scorer. (Do not eat the cocktail sticks!)

MAKING THINGS TO SELL

Advertising and Marketing: If you plan to make small items for people your own age, the best place to sell them will be at school. If you make jewellery, wear a sample *every* day; each time someone admires it you will have an opportunity to sell one. *Give* your best friend one but persuade him or her to pretend to buy it from you in front of a crowd of other kids. You could start a fashion trend and get lots of orders.

Friendship Bracelets

A friendship bracelet is a very special present. It tells someone you really like them. Worn all the time, it is only taken off when a friendship is over. There are times when a bracelet does have to be taken off so its owner can swim, bathe, or wash up, but of course a friendship will easily survive that! They are popular with both boys and girls, from quite young children to mid-teenagers.

You Will Need

3 (8-metre) skeins of embroidery cotton (bright colours); or woollen thread

Masking tape, or safety pin
Scissors
Ruler or tape measure

Makes: approximately 250 bracelets
Time: 5 minutes per bracelet
Approximate cost: 50p per skein (x 3 = £1.50)
Selling price: 20p per bracelet
Need to Sell: 8 bracelets to cover expenses. Each one you make after that, will earn you 20p profit.

Embroidery threads have the best colours and can be bought in craft shops and department stores. You might even find some in the family's sewing basket, and there's often some for sale very cheaply at car-boot and jumble sales. Once you've made one you will be able to make them without looking. You can watch TV as you work, if you secure the threads to your jeans with a safety pin.

Simple Plait Friendship Bracelet

1. Take three 30 cm (12 in) lengths of different brightly coloured threads.
2. Tie the threads together with a knot about 3 cm (1 in)

from one end (this will form a short tassel).

3. Tape the knot to a work surface (not the priceless antique dining table!) or sit down and pin it to your jeans just above the knee. Imagine-label the threads as A, B, and C.

4. Lift A over B, so A becomes the centre thread and the threads are arranged as B-A-C.

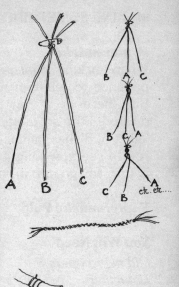

5. Lift C over A into the centre, and now the threads will be arranged as B-C-A. Repeat this, left to the centre, right to the centre until your plait is long enough to fit comfortably around your wrist (or your little sister's if you're aiming for a younger market).

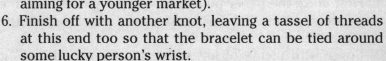

6. Finish off with another knot, leaving a tassel of threads at this end too so that the bracelet can be tied around some lucky person's wrist.

There are ways of *knotting* lovely and rather more complicated friendship bracelets. If you want to try making them, go to a library and look in the children's craft section for books with instructions and diagrams.

MAKING SOMETHING FROM NOTHING

Papier-mâché
When making *papier-mâché* objects you need time and patience to let it dry out before applying another layer! But, here is a relatively quick method. Once you've mastered the art of *papier-mâché* you can use it to make all kinds of dishes, animal ornaments and jewellery. Do a test run to see how long it takes you and work out your costs before you go into production.

Papier-mâché Pulp

You Will Need
Old newspapers	An airtight plastic container
Hot water	with a lid
An old plastic bowl	Rubber gloves

1. First make the paper pulp. Wear rubber gloves, tear the paper into 3 cm (1 in) wide strips and place them in the plastic bowl.
2. Cover with plenty of hot water and let it soak until it becomes mushy. Stir it occasionally.
3. Scoop the pulp out of the bowl, squeeze out any extra water, and transfer it to a plastic container, ready to use.

Papier-mâché Piggy Bank
Based on Juliet Bawden's *Making Presents* (Hamlyn).

A piggy bank is an essential item for anyone saving money at home, so you should be able to sell them to friends and other kids at school. The following costing is left blank for you to fill in. Time yourself (allow

5p per minute for your time), work out how much the piggy bank cost you to make, then deduct your costs from the selling price to work out your profit.

Time to make:	
Approx. cost to make:	
Selling price:	
Profit:	

You Will Need

A small balloon
Newspaper, torn into
  3 cm (1") wide strips
PVA glue and water
Bowl of paper pulp (see
  page 52)
5 corks and a pin
Masking tape

Thin card, cut into two
  pig's ears
Scissors
Dustbin tie
Poster or acrylic paints
Brush
Paper varnish (water
  soluble)

1. Blow up the balloon and tie the end in a knot. Brush glue on to the strips of paper and stick them all over the balloon.
2. Leave to dry before applying a thick layer of paper pulp.

Set aside to dry. When it is dry, paste on another layer of paper strips.

3. Burst the balloon with the pin. Cut one cork in half for the nose and glue it on to the *papier-mâché* sphere. Hold it in place with the masking tape.

4. Glue and tape on the other four corks for the legs. Cut a thin rectangular hole in the top, big enough for money to go through. Cut two slits for the ears you have cut out of cardboard.

5. Now coat the sphere with two more layers of glued newspaper strips, allowing the first layer to dry out before applying the next.

6. When completely dry, add an undercoat of white then paint over it in pink. Finally, add the features of the pig's face in black.

7. Allow to dry, before giving the piggy bank a final coat of varnish. Clean all your brushes and put everything away.

SEWING THINGS TO SELL

Teddybear Bean Bags

These little teddies are irresistible and great to make just big enough to hold in your hand. When you cut your pattern make sure the arms and legs are quite thick otherwise it will not be possible to turn the teddy inside-out after you've stitched all around it.

Time: 20-30 minutes.
Cost price: Possibly free if you have materials!

Selling price: 75p
Profit: 75p (or 50p if you allow 25p for time)

You Will Need

Pencil and paper   *Needle*
Newspaper   *Cotton-wool, dried beans or*
Scissors   *lentils*
Fake fur fabric   *Embroidery thread or wool*
Pins

1. To make a pattern, draw the shape of a little teddy on a piece of paper. Cut it out.
2. Pin it to two pieces of fabric that have their right (patterned) sides facing each other.
3. Cut the fabric around the teddy pattern. Pin the two pieces of fabric together (right sides inwards). Sew a line of stitching about 1 cm (0.7 in) in from the edge nearly all the way round. Leave a small gap in your stitching so you can turn the teddy inside-out through it.
4. Fill the teddy with lentils or any small beans. Slip-stitch the opening up.
5. Sew on the ears, eyes and mouth with the embroidery thread or wool.

Sewing Things for Free
You can sew many other presents (to sell) using the same method as used to make the teddybears. That is, sew two pieces of material together with their right sides facing inwards, then turn them inside out and stuff them with beans, or something soft like kapok or cotton wool.

    You can even make fragrant spelling heart-shaped cushions

by filling them with lavender or dried herbs.

Most households have some old clothes or curtains that can be cut up and made into scarves, cushions or soft toys. Or you could cut up old towels and make them into funny face-cloths.

MODELLING THINGS TO SELL

Ornaments Made Out of Salt Dough

Salt dough is simple to make and easy to turn into lots of things to sell. Model it into anything you think other kids will want to buy. It makes good Christmas tree decorations, doll's house furniture, doll's cups and saucers, or toy fruit and vegetables that you could use in a toy grocery shop or to decorate picture frames.

Write down how long it takes you to make.

Time to make:	
Approx. cost to make:	
Selling price:	
Profit:	

You Will Need

Ingredients

2 cups plain flour

1 cup salt

1 cup cold water

2 tbls cooking oil

Food colouring (optional)

Egg yolk (optional)

Aluminium foil

Baking tray

Acrylic paints

1. Set the oven to 150°C (300°F) or gas mark 2. Line a baking tray with foil.
2. Mix the ingredients together until they form into a ball. Knead this dough until it becomes soft and pliable. You can leave it plain or colour it with food colouring.
3. Model your dough into any shape you want, then lay it in the baking tray. If you want your models to have a shiny yellow gloss, brush them with egg yolk before they are baked. Or, alternatively, paint them with other colours after they are baked. Bake for 1 hour, or until they are completely hard.
4. Wear an oven glove to remove them and set aside to cool completely before painting.

Tricks of the Trade

- Press some of the dough through a garlic crusher to make strands of hair or prickles.
- Stick a matchstick in the dough to make a hole in the top before you bake it. Then you'll be able to thread a ribbon through it and hang it up.
- Use cutlery to give your models texture.
- You can add lots of details by sticking on extra dough with a dab of water before you bake it.
- Stick a magnet on the back with some glue after they've been painted, to make fridge magnets.

Advertising and Marketing: You could have a Christmas craft party at home and invite all your friends to bring things to sell or barter (see page 31). You can market salt dough Christmas decorations from October to mid December by distributing flyers in your neighbourhood. Also at Christmas fairs at school or in the church hall.

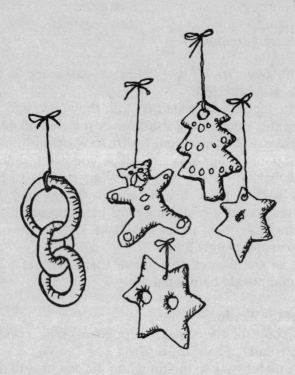

Chapter Six

GROWING THINGS TO SELL

Do you have green fingers? No, not *really*. Someone who has green fingers is a person who finds it easy to grow plants. It's the next best thing to being a magician. You take a tiny wizened seed or bulb, put it in some potting

compost, add water and, hey presto! A few days later an entirely new and fresh green plant will shoot up to greet you. With a few basic gardening skills you could very soon have a thriving business.

Even with a limited amount of space like a sunny windowsill or tower block balcony, you could grow seedlings in small pots to sell. If you have a garden, you could grow vegetables and fruits and sell the fresh produce. If your garden already has apple, pear or cherry trees in it and they produce more fruit than your family can eat, you could pick and sell them to neighbours, or even make delicious fruit pies to sell.

Gardening may take a lot of time altogether but it is spread out over weeks so that you can easily do it if you can spare only half an hour a day.

Something for Nothing

Anyone who likes plants is sure to have stacks of old flower pots and would gladly give them to you. Ask your neighbours if they would like you to recycle theirs; or distribute a leaflet, saying you will call by on a certain afternoon to collect any unwanted flower pots or gardening materials.

Give a few days warning to allow people to dig them out! Be sure to turn up on the day you say you will. No adult will be pleased to have scrabbled around in the dust and cobwebs of their garage for nothing. Remember they could be your potential customers so you need to keep them sweet!

If you can't afford to buy seeds, you can gather them free at the end of summer and store them in a cool dry place ready to plant the next spring. Start looking at flowers and see how each one makes their seeds in different ways. When the flower head is dried out, simply shake it over your palm and you will have plenty of seeds for next year. Try growing the pips from oranges and apples. Collect acorns and chestnuts once they've fallen to the ground and start your own tree farm.

Advertising and Marketing
See chapter four. If you choose to make and distribute flyers, they could be very attractively decorated with drawings of leaves and fruits. If you would rather make a collage, cut out pictures of luscious looking fruit, vegetables and flowers from old magazines or from your seed packets.

People are especially glad to be able to buy fruit and vegetables that have not been sprayed with any poisons. If you can claim that your produce is free of any pesticides, it would be a very good selling point to include on your advertising flyer.

If you live in a village that has a local Women's Institute market day, you could run a stall during the summer holidays to sell either plants or your fruit and vegetable produce. Or, you and your friends could set up a stall in your front garden. Make big signs to attract attention. Write them clearly so that people can see instantly what you are doing and what the prices are. Even adults can sometimes be too shy to ask. Don't forget to work out your costing (see page 25) before deciding how much to charge for your plants or produce.

Lots of adults love plants but do not always have time to go to the trouble of planting seeds and looking after little seedlings. The market is out there, you just have to find it.

How to Get Started

Plants can be grown from seeds, cuttings or bulbs. If you don't have a garden with a ready supply of good soil or compost, you will need to spend some money to get started – but not much, and, like the plants, the money you spend will soon start growing. As long as you take good care of your little plants and find people to buy them you will certainly make a profit. If you like the idea of growing vegetables it would be a good idea to get a specialist book from the library that gives step-by-step instructions. Whichever method you choose to grow your plants, you are going to need some basic equipment.

You Will Need
Small bag John Innes No 2 potting compost
Small plastic pots (recycled if possible)
Labels (cut up plastic food cartons)
Pencil or waterproof pen
Plant food (such as Baby Bio)
Fork and trowel (borrow them if possible)
A gardening book from the library

SAMPLE COSTING (To grow 50+ seedlings)
1 packet seeds: approximately £1.00
Small bag John Innes No. 2 Compost: £2.20
Plant Food: £1.20
Total expenses: £4.40 (= 9p per plant)
Time: Lots, but it's worth it. The time is difficult to estimate because looking after growing plants is spread out over weeks. Say 6p per plant.
Total cost per plant: 15p
Selling price: 35p–50p per plant (depends on size)
Profit: 20p–35p per plant (x 50 = £10–£17.50!)

Take my Advice!
If you're gardening inside, cover the table with
newspaper *before* you start.

Growing Flowers for Outdoors
Just some of the many brightly coloured flowers that
are easy to grow from seed are nasturtiums, wallflowers,

poppies, sunflowers, and sweetpeas. You will find many more packets of seeds on sale at garden centres or in supermarkets in spring. Choose the ones you like but read the instructions on the packet carefully to check what time of year the seeds should be sown and any other advice. You need to be sure you can provide the right environment for your plants.

Indoor Plants

There are many indoor plants to choose from that are really easy to grow from cuttings, such as busy lizzy, ivy, geraniums, umbrella grass, striped inch plant, spider plants.

One of the most spectacularly beautiful flowers that grows very easily from a bulb (simply planted in compost and watered) is an Amaryllis. They make marvellous gifts so would be easy to sell. A ready-to-grow bulb, pot and compost kit can cost between £4–£5 in the shops.

Hyacinths are also grown from bulbs and when in flower will fill a room with a delightful scent (plant three in one pot). If you buy your bulbs loose from a garden centre you could easily undercut your competitors' prices.

To get your friends interested in buying plants, your best advertisement will be to grow a jungle in your own room. It's very easy and most indoor plants will survive quite happily even if you sometimes forget to water them. Many actually prefer to dry out before being watered. But, do remember to open the curtains every day because the plants will need light.

Growing Food

If the summer is hot and you remember to water and feed them, some plants like runner beans, tomatoes and courgettes will produce masses and masses of fresh vegetables or fruits. It might be the easiest thing in the world to sell your home-grown vegetables because they are so delicious your parents will want to eat them all. And they will very happily pay you for them, especially if they cost even a penny less than in the supermarket.

There is always a market for herbs that are used in cookery, such as rosemary, mint, chives, parsley or thyme. They can all be grown from seeds, and rosemary can be grown from cuttings. You can sell the plants as well as keeping some for yourself. As they grow bigger you will be able to dry the leaves to sell as dried herbs in pretty little packets.

Growing from Seeds

Read the sowing instructions on your seed packet in case your chosen plant has any special needs. Otherwise, most seeds will germinate if you:

1. Pierce holes in the bottoms of some plastic food containers (like margarine tubs); or use seed trays or small plastic flower pots.

2. Fill the containers with compost; sprinkle on your seeds and press them gently into the compost so they are just covered.
3. Water each container and cover with some plastic (a piece of old plastic bag will do) so that the seeds will be kept damp and warm. They will germinate in a few days. Some seeds germinate quicker if they are first soaked in luke warm water for a few hours. Label each pot with the name of the plant, especially if you are planting more than one variety, otherwise you won't know which is which when you come to sell them.
4. Put the containers in a warm dark place and check each day that the compost is still moist. Only add water if it looks as if it is drying out.
5. As soon as some shoots appear above the soil, remove the plastic covering and put the containers on a sunny windowsill. When the plants have grown about 5 cm (2 in) tall, gently remove each and replant it in its own little pot.
6. Give them a little plant food (according to the instructions on the label) and keep them watered until they look big enough to leave you and survive on their own with a new carer!

Growing from a Cutting
One of the best things about growing a plant from a cutting is that you don't have to wait a long time before you have a plant. A good plant to grow from a cutting is a geranium. You will, of course need a fully grown plant to take a cutting from. They are often on sale at summer fairs or car-boot sales.

1. Gently pull a strong healthy side shoot away from the main stem so that it has a kind of heel at its base.
2. Plant the cutting in a pot of compost. Pull off the lower leaves and any dead leaves. Press the soil around the

stem firmly and gently. Water it.

3. Keep it on a sunny windowsill and water it just enough to keep the soil damp. It will soon grow into a sturdy plant. You can grow geranium cuttings outside too but check them every day and water them as often as necessary to keep the soil just damp.

Not all cuttings are successful, so take a number of cuttings from your original plant. The more you take, the more new plants you will have to sell. Lots of plants will grow by this method but find a book in the library about propagation if you'd like to experiment with other plants and methods.

Growing plants from bulbs
Some bulbs need to be planted in winter and may take about 8–10 weeks before they flower.

You Will Need
Bulbs (try daffodils or hyacinths)
Bulb fibre
Pebbles (or bits of broken clay pots)

1. Use plant pots with a drainage hole. Put a layer of pebbles in the bottom of it to help any excess water drain away. Your bulbs could rot if they're sitting in a puddle all the time.
2. Fill each pot with bulb fibre and soak in water for 1 hour. Squeeze out any excess moisture.
3. If you have big pots, plant a number of bulbs in each. Plant them with the green shoot sticking up. The shoulders of a hyacinth bulb should show just above the surface of the compost. But only the nose of a daffodil should be visible.
4. Put the pots somewhere dark and cool, such as a shed but don't forget to water them regularly to keep the

compost slightly damp.

5. When leaves start appearing (maybe 8 weeks later), move the pots to a lighter place. The best time to sell them is when flower buds have emerged so that they will come into flower very soon after your customer has bought them.

Chapter Seven

RECYCLING, COLLECTING AND INVENTING

RECYCLING

You've got to tidy your room – you can't put it off any longer or you'll have to sleep on the roof! Before you chuck out your old toys or clothes to make room for new ones – STOP! You may be able to make some money from them. Some things, like toys and comics, will actually be worth more than they originally cost, as long as they're in good condition and you keep them long enough.

Before you sell anything, check with your mum or dad that it's OK. They probably bought lots of your things for you and might not want you to sell them. Also, they will make sure you don't sell your stuff too cheaply. Try not to sell things that you could *give* to a younger brother or sister.

Good Places to Sell Anything Secondhand:

Car-boot and garage sales (do it with an adult or friend); secondhand, collectors' or bric-a-brac markets (ask stall-holders if they would be interested in buying your stuff); secondhand book- or clothes shops (not charity shops); school and local fairs (ones where you pay for your pitch but keep your profits); jumble sales; markets.

If you want to have your own stall at a fair or market, you may have to pay for your pitch. Make sure you have enough things to sell to cover your expenses. Sell things you've made as well. It would be more fun to have a stall with a friend and they could share the cost. Offer to sell things for other friends and charge them a small commission. Stick price labels on all your sales items; some people don't like to ask about prices.

You will also need to have plenty of change. If a customer wants your dad's jacket for £8 but he only has a £20 note, you might miss out on a big sale if you don't have any change. Wear a money belt to keep your dosh safe. And if anyone tries to snatch it, let them have the money rather than risk getting yourself hurt.

For large or more expensive items, such as bikes, the old climbing frame, computer games, etc., it might be better to advertise in a free-ads paper like *Loot*. Also, the ads in it will give you an idea of how much you can charge for second-hand goods. You can advertise in the local newspaper, put a card in the newsagent's window or on the noticeboard at a superstore.

Many things can be recycled for a profit. You'll know what can be bought and sold in the school playground but here are some other ideas.

Old Books

If you don't want your old books any more and they are in a good condition, you might be able to sell them. Give the rest away to a charity shop. Or, phone your dentist or doctor's surgery to see if they would like them for kids to read in the waiting room.

Old Clothes

Old clothes can be profitable. You can't sell any that are dirty or have holes in them, and you'll get better prices if they're all freshly ironed.

Sort out the things you no longer wear (and that your mum doesn't want you to pass on to your younger brother or sister!). Look under *Secondhand dealers* in the *Yellow Pages* to find your nearest secondhand clothes shop. Before you traipse down there with a heavy bag of old football shorts and baby clothes, ring to ask if the shop is interested in what you have. If there's a big bagful, try charming your mum or dad into giving you a lift in the car. If your dazzling charm fails, try bartering a service with them. Your parents may even let you have some old clothes they no longer want. If your dad's old sheepskin jacket or your mum's seventies dress is back in fashion, they'd sell for good prices.

Bad Clothes to Sell: smelly trainers, underpants, holey socks, single socks, stretched T-shirts with nasty dribbly stains, pyjamas.

Good Clothes to Sell: coats, jeans, dresses, hats, suits, sports clothes, jackets, Wellington boots, skirts, trousers, party clothes (they usually cost a lot and won't have been worn very often).

Old Toys

Tucked away on the top of your wardrobe or in that long undisturbed dusty corner under your bed, you might come across some old toys you've forgotten about. There could be jigsaws, games, old teddybears, dolls, Dinky toys – all sorts of things. As long as they are in *good condition* (no pieces missing from jigsaws or games; dolls have their two arms, legs and eyes; etc.), they will sell.

Old Action Men (as long as they haven't been too

tortured), Barbie dolls and toy cars can all fetch extraordinary prices, so if you've got some that still look good, get on down to your nearest collectors' market. Stallholders will, of course, pay you much less than they are charging on their stall. Check out what else is being sold while you're there. You'll be amazed.

CREATIVE RECYCLING

In the poorer countries of the developing world very little is wasted. In Mexico City the poorest children live on what they can find in the rubbish tips. In Africa, people make all sorts of things to sell from stuff that we just throw away without a thought. Bottle tops are made into bags. Old pieces of wire are twisted and wound into sculptures. Jewellery is made from scraps of wood, cork, old drink cans, and coconut shells. Fantastic toys and ornaments are made from any kind of old tin can.

Your household probably throws away many things that could be creatively recycled into something to sell. Old boxes could be decorated with shells that you collected at the beach last summer. You could make earrings from old corks or small coloured bottle tops (smooth-edged ones). Delightful Christmas decorations and mobiles can be made from flattened milk bottle tops or tinfoil food containers. Fir cones can be collected in the woods and sprayed gold and silver to sell as Christmas ornaments. Horse manure can be sold to people you garden for. In Central Park, New York City, where tourists can ride in horse-drawn carriages, people collect the manure for their window boxes. If your dad is a keen handyman, you could offer to sweep up the sawdust in his workshop (he might even pay you to do it!). Sell bags of it to people to put on the bottom of the cages of their pet gerbils or hamsters. Whenever you see anything being thrown away, try to imagine something you could make with it.

COLLECTING

The Bad News is: Building up a collection takes time and patience. Most valuable collections have taken many years to acquire and if you want to collect something like every aluminium drink can ever produced, then you must have the space to store them.

The Good News is: It can be great fun. You can meet lots of other people who are interested in the same thing as you. There are collectors' clubs you can join, and while you are collecting you are learning all the time. You could become a world expert on whatever it is you choose to collect.

One of the most important things about collecting is the condition of the items. They have to be undamaged to be of any *real* value. If you have kept the original packaging, and it's in mint condition too, one single Dinky toy may one day be worth hundreds of pounds.

Something else that makes a collection valuable is how comprehensive it is. For example, if you could get hold of every kind of telephone card that has ever been produced you would have a very saleable and interesting collection.

It doesn't really matter what it is, there will be someone somewhere collecting it. If you need inspiration to start your own *priceless collection,* have a look at this list of some of things other people collect: football cards; stamps; telephone cards; books; postcards; matchboxes; coins; comics; records; CDs; tapes; old radios; potties; posters; toys; toy trains and cars; games; dolls, doll's houses and furniture; sports memorabilia such as kit, team strips,

programmes and entrance tickets; cinema tickets; pop concert memorabilia such as tickets, posters, T-shirts, etc.; teapots; honey jars; teaspoons; beer mats; key rings; bottle tops; corn flake packets, etc.

You can never really be sure that what you decide to collect will one day be valuable. The best idea is to enjoy collecting something that really interests you. If one day you can sell it, that will be an extra bonus.

INVENTING

Everything we use has been invented by someone and some of the simplest ideas have made people millionaires. For example, ball point pens, cat's eyes (that reflect a car's headlights to show where the middle of the road is), milk cartons, spill-proof mugs for toddlers, and zips.

A good inventor might invent something entirely new, or will see an everyday task and realize that there is an easier or more efficient way to do it. It may be as simple as coating the end of a shoelace with plastic to make it easier for you to lace your shoes in the morning; or as complicated as a computer or fax machine. If you come up with an invention, you're sure it works (and your parents agree it is nothing short of BRILLIANT), the first thing you have to do is to patent the invention so that no one else can steal the idea. It is very expensive to take out a patent, but, who knows, your solution to a problem could end up making you lots of dosh! If you think you've got a winner, ring the Patent Office (Department of Trade) and ask for details of how to go about it. Phone: 0171 438 4700.

Chapter Eight

PROVIDING SERVICES

Job Specifications and Quotes, Services to Offer

If you don't like making things, offering your services is also a good way to make money. You can use your time and skills to provide a service doing something for someone who doesn't want to do it, or can't, and who is willing to pay you to do it. A good place to begin is at home. Your house works a little like a service industry.

Take my Advice!
Some jobs around the house you do simply because you are a member of a family. Don't even think about charging for them. Imagine if your parents started charging you for their services!

Work out with your parents a list of what they expect you do around the house or garden as a matter of course, such as tidying your room and helping with day-to-day chores like the washing-up, clearing the table, or walking *your* dog!

Then make a list of the jobs that are *not* your specific responsibility and that no one else ever *wants* to do. These are the ones where you can make money while providing a really useful service. The more obnoxious or boring the job, the more money you can charge for doing it. Every family will come up with a different list but see pages 16–20 for plenty of suggestions for both indoor and outdoor jobs.

Once you've tested and practised your skills on your long-suffering family, you can offer your services to neighbours or other people your parents know and trust. Always tell your parents what, when and where you are planning to do any jobs outside your own home.

If you start doing a number of tasks for different people, it is essential to draw up a timetable so that you don't forget (see pages 27–29). Plan in the time you need for your homework, seeing your friends and enjoying your hobbies, etc.

Reliability

Remember, before you offer any services whether it is at home or for other people, you will have to be reliable. Whatever service you intend to do, it will have to be done at the time you have agreed to and done properly – even if it's a yukky job and you just want to get it over and done with. Otherwise, people will not employ you again.

JOB SPECIFICATIONS AND QUOTES

When you offer a service to someone you will have to know what you are going to charge them. Go back to Chapter Three (page 23) to see how to work out your costing. You will need to be able to assess how much time and equipment you will need to do a job, then give your customer an estimate of how much you will charge. Some people will want a written estimate (or quote).

When quoting for a job you must state *exactly* what you will do for how much money. For example, a quote for tidying up and sorting out a bookshelf might look like this:

JOB SPECIFICATION AND ESTIMATE

JOB: Tidying up and sorting out TWO bookshelves in the sitting room.

DATE & TIME: Sunday 10th, 4–6 p.m.

1. Remove all books from the shelves.
2. Dust and wipe the bookshelves clean.
3. Arrange books back on the shelves by size.

PRICE: £4.50 not including dusting the books.

DUSTING THE BOOKS, EXTRA: £2.50

OTHER SERVICES TO OFFER

Sorting out/labelling videos: 50p–£1 per hour.
If most of the videos are unlabelled you'll need to fast-forward a lot or it will take so much time you'll have to charge more than anyone will ever be willing to pay you.

Sorting out photographs: 50p–£1 per hour.
Sort into date order and put photos into albums.

Morning Tea and Wake-up Call: 15p per day.
You might need an alarm clock (or two) to get yourself up in the morning. If anyone depends on you to get them up in time for work or school, you must *never* let them down! If your older brother doesn't have any money, your parents might be willing to pay you so they don't have the bother of getting him up.

Tidying brother or sister's room: £1 per hour.
With practice you'll know how long it will take you, so be

sure to warn them how expensive it will be if their room is a total tip, and charge extra for dealing with such things as festering football socks and disgustingly smelly trainers. You can always offer to barter (see page 31) your work in return for something you want from them.

Ironing: 25p per shirt; 25p a sheet.
Boring, I know. But, that's exactly why people would pay you to do it. You can always listen to music or the radio while you work.

General Housework: dusting, vacuuming, changing bed linen and making beds
Suggested Service Charges:
£2.50 to vacuum a whole house.
50p to dust a sitting room.
50p per bed to change sheets and put used ones out for washing.
5–10p to make a bed with a duvet.
15p to make a bed with blankets.

Any work that has to be repeated every day or each week is a drag for the person who has to do it. They're usually very pleased to pay someone else to do it. Housework is good weekend work. But don't forget if you're being paid,

the job must be done well – no skirting around the chairs and ornaments, everything must be cleaned and that involves lifting and moving things!

Take my Advice!
Put on some music and dance your way through boring jobs. Or set yourself a competition and try to do the job faster and faster every week.

Helping With Homework: £1.50 per hour.
You'll need a good brain. Only offer this service if you are good at schoolwork. You won't last long if your students don't get top marks!

Practise on your younger brothers and sisters before offering your skills to children outside the family. You can charge other parents a bit more!

Take my Advice!
Don't take on students unless you can *really* help them;
nor if they are smarter than you!
Praise children for what they can do, or know, and
gently encourage them to understand more.

Window Cleaning: 50p–75p per window.
This job has good business potential for when you're older. Offer your services to neighbours and work as a team with some friends, but stick to cleaning low windows or the insides (you could offer to clean mirrors at the same time). High external windows are definitely *off limits*.

You Will Need
A bucket
Window cleaner, or soapy water and a rubber window squeegee

A soft clean cloth to dry polish the windows and mirrors
Small step ladder (maybe)

Advertising and marketing: The sparkling windows of your own house will be your best advertisement. Put a sign in the front window. Drum up business with a flyer (see page 38). Your eye-catching headlines might read:

Seeing the world through a grimy haze?
LET LIGHT INTO YOUR LIFE!
Phone:
Johnny & Jo's
WINDOW CLEANING SERVICES

Guarantee to wash windows cheaper than any competitor. When you're older and really good at it, you can ask at local shops if they want their windows washed. Shop fronts tend to be quite high though! A good time to canvass for window cleaning jobs is just after a storm.

Cleaning Shoes: at home 10p–20p a pair. Outside customers: 25p–40p per pair.

This is a quick and easy way to make money. Begin by cleaning shoes for the family twice a week, say, on Sunday and Tuesday evenings. Then, if there are lots of passers-by, you can set up a shoe shining service in the front garden. If you do it at a regular time *every* weekend, your neighbours might be glad to bring round all their shoes for a polish. Make a clear sign stating your prices.

You Will Need

Some newspaper	*Chair for customers*
Shoe polish (selection	*Box to put their feet on*
of colours)	*Cushion for you to kneel on*
Rags and brushes	

Special skills: Be friendly and quick. The faster you work, the more money you can make. Don't get any polish on a customer's socks!

Bubble or Scented Baths: 10p per bath.

What could be better than having a warm scented bubble bath ready to relax into after a hard day at the office or school? This service could be a real treat. If you don't want to charge your family, it's an excellent service to barter with. If you're paying for the bath oils, don't forget to add a proportion of the cost to your service charge.

Dog Beauty Parlour:
£2.50 to shampoo a dog.
Dogs do pong sometimes and occasionally need a bath and brushing. This is a very useful service to offer if you like animals. It's easier and even more fun if you work with a friend.

You Will Need
A *dog lead*
Dog shampoo
Hose
Yard or garden
Old towels
Dog brush and comb
Dog biscuits as a reward (or bribe!)

Dog washing is definitely more of a spring and summer job. It's too cold in the winter for both you and the dog. It's best to wash a dog outside, as your parents or other dog owners may be furious if you do it in the bathroom. Ask the owner what method their dog is used to. Few dogs like being washed so make sure they're friendly and play with them for a few minutes *before* you start! And afterwards, give the dog a reward – for not biting!

Advertising and Marketing: You could tie a notice advertising the service on your own (very clean) dog's back when you take it for walks. You could post advertising flyers through the doors of friendly dog owners who your parents know.

Take my Advice!
Rinse out and dry the towels after dog washing because damp towels left in the dirty washing basket will soon start to reek. Wear old clothes – you might end up having a bath too!

Cleaning Out Pets' Cages: £2–£5 per cage.

No one could actually *like* cleaning out the cage of their hamster, gerbil, rat, mouse, budgie or stick insect. It is definitely a *gold star* service, that is EXPENSIVE. You can adjust your charge, depending on whose pet it is and how long since the cage was last cleaned.

You Will Need

Rubber gloves
Newspaper
Plastic bags
Old rags

Nose peg (optional)
Box to keep the pet in
    during the cleaning

Cage cleaning is worth *a lot* of credit points if you are bartering services with a brother or sister. Always get them to do what you want done *first*. Remember, you're the business *brain*.

Take my Advice!
Ask the pet owner what is the best way to clean out the cage and how to handle the animal safely.

Holiday Pet Care
You could offer to look after small pets in your own home during the holidays, but ask your parents' permission first.

Or, you could arrange to feed a cat whenever your neighbours are away. Make sure you get adequate instructions and a key to the house, and also ask the pet owner to get in enough food to last for the number of days they are going to be away.

Take my Advice!

If you go on holiday, let people know in advance when you will not be able to work. They will be relying on you and will have to make other arrangements. On holiday you spend money, not earn it; so remember to budget for that.

Party Helper: £2–£2.50 per person per hour.

If your parents, other relatives, or neighbours are planning

to have a party, offer your expert services (see pages 33–34).

Being a party helper at home is an excellent way to gain experience before you are old enough to apply for part-time jobs such as working in restaurants or as a cinema usher. You could even start a business offering to do all the preparation for parties.

Group Activity: It is fun to work with friends when you are helping out at parties. And you won't have to work so hard.

Business Potential: Start a party-helpers agency. Arrange for friends to do the work, advertise the service by distributing flyers, and take a small percentage of your workers' wages to pay you for doing all the organization.

Advertising and Marketing: Word-of-mouth recommendations and flyers through known and trusted neighbours' letterboxes.

Take my Advice!
Only offer party services at weekends or during the school holidays. If the party is in the evening, charge for the cost of a taxi home.

Children's Party Organizer and Entertainer

Young children's parties need plenty of helpers. They can be chaotic if not well organized.

Essential Skills Required: You must enjoy playing with and making small children laugh; maybe even have a clown's outfit or be able to make funny faces! Know how to organize games.

Service Charge: Most parties last from 2–3 hours including the tea. You may need to be there to help prepare the food and going-home sweetie bags, or just for helping out during the party and teatime, so charge for your time plus extra for any special skills. The larger the party, the more you should charge as you may need to pay a helper. Agree with whoever is giving the party how much you can charge (minimum of £1.50 per hour). Don't forget it's good to give your services free for your favourite little kids.

Advertising and Marketing: Everyone who attends a party is a potential customer, or their parents are. Hand out leaflets at each party or give each child a tiny present with your address and telephone number on it when they go home.

Party Entertainer: £2–£5 per hour (or as noted).
Look under *Entertainers* in the *Yellow Pages* to see the kind of amusements professional entertainers offer. To check your competitors' prices, ring and ask them for a quote. You are bound to be able to do your own version of some entertainments a lot cheaper than the professionals.

Face Painting: 50p per face.
You can paint children's faces at parties, fairs, or carnivals,

using special face paints. Most kids love having their faces painted and will drag their parents over to you. You might have to bribe your own little brother or sister to be your first customer!

You Will Need

Non-toxic, water-soluble face paints (about £1).

A book in which you have drawn some face designs for the children to choose from.

A mirror for the children to see how they look.

A camera (optional) If you have one, take a photo of each child to use in future advertising.

Match your face designs to the occasion. For example, at Easter fairs draw rabbit faces; for Hallowe'en do ghouls, ghosts and witches; and at carnivals and birthday parties draw clowns or any kind of happy animal faces.

Special Skills: Good at drawing and painting.

Potential Business: Offer face painting as part of your party helper service.

Party Photographer

You Will Need

A *camera with a flash*	*Enough money to have the*
Colour film	*film developed*

Proud parents can't resist photographs of their kids, especially when they're all dressed up. And little children love to have their photos taken. Always take more than one photo of each child in case one doesn't come out! Ask the host or hostess of the party if they would like you to take photos, then give them a quote. First, find out how much it will cost to buy the film and have the prints made. Divide that by the number of prints on your film to find out how much each print will cost you. You could charge double that amount for a good photograph.

Disc Jockey: £10+ per hour.
This is a real plum of a job for anyone who loves music. For parties you will need a record deck, cassette or CD player with some good speakers (and a microphone if it's to be held in a public hall) and, as well as a large record or tape collection. Under *Disco Equipment* in the *Yellow Pages* you will find companies that hire out music equipment. Ring some near you to check prices for renting. You will also need a sympathetic parent to drive you and the equipment about and maybe lend you some money to get started.

Service Charge: As this will be very costly to set up you must do your costing very carefully and get your customer's approval of your quote before you start renting equipment. Or if you and your friends are setting up a party venue and charging an entrance fee, sell tickets first so you can be sure to cover your expenses and make a profit. This will take up a lot of time. Apart from organizing the equipment, you will need about 30 minutes at least to set up, the party will usually last about four hours plus another 30–45 minutes to pack away and leave the premises as clean and tidy as you found them. Charge at least £10 per hour for your time at the party.

Marketing and Advertising: Put up a notice at school, libraries, or in any youth clubs you go to. You could also put a classified ad in your local newspaper or distribute flyers. Have plenty of flyers advertising your services and give them out after the party. If you're selling tickets, you could offer discounts for large bookings.

Special Skills: You need to have a lively outgoing personality and be able to get people to enjoy themselves. As you get some experience you will see how the kind of music you select can affect the mood of the party. You will also need very good organizational skills.

MORE INDOOR JOBS

Plant Watering Service: 50p–£1 per visit.
This is a great service to offer people who go out to work or who travel a lot.
Special Skills: Read up about house plants and find out what conditions they like and how often to water each variety you are caring for. Your client will probably know what they need and give you instructions, but they will be very impressed if you obviously know about what plants need.

You Will Need
A fine-spray watering can for indoor plants
Plant food (such as Baby Bio, approx. £1.20)
Damp cloth to keep leaves dust-free

Make a timetable (see page 28) to keep track of when you have to check each customer's plants. Ask each of your clients to fill in a checklist so that you have a record of what care each of their plants needs. Here is an example of how a checklist might look:

ROSIE'S PLANT WATERING SERVICE

Phone: 123 4567

Client's Name: ....

Address: ....

Phone No.: ....

PLANT NAME	POSITION IN HOUSE	WHEN TO WATER	SPECIAL NEEDS
Cacti.	Top of stairs.	Once a month.	Let soil dry out. Water into dish under pot.

Silver Polishing Service: £1–£2 per hour.

Not many people have silver to polish but those who do will always welcome someone willing to polish it for them, especially before a special occasion like Christmas. Open the window to ventilate the room while you work so you don't breathe in the fumes.

You Will Need

Rubber gloves
Silver polish
Old newspaper

Old rags
Soft cloth or duster

Cover the work surface with newspaper before you start. Rub on the silver polish with a rag then use a duster to polish it off. Keep the silver in plastic bags once it is polished.

Marketing and Advertising: Just before holidays such as Christmas or Easter, distribute flyers in your neighbourhood, offering lots of different services. For example you could work out a Christmas present wrapping service for busy people.

Computers: £5–£10 per hour.

If you're a computer whiz kid, you could help technologically backward adults find their way around their computer systems. You could teach them to surf the Internet or how to open up a Web-site on it. Try hard not to sound too amazed at how little they know. They will be eternally grateful for encouraging and patient advice.

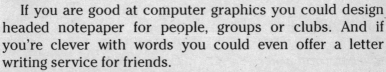

If you are good at computer graphics you could design headed notepaper for people, groups or clubs. And if you're clever with words you could even offer a letter writing service for friends.

If you're a fast and accurate typist you could advertise a typing service for essays, letters, notices, other people's advertising flyers, etc.

If you have about £20 to invest you could buy a large

quantity of computer disks and sell them individually to friends for a little more than you paid for each one. Do some research first to make sure there are enough people who use the same kind of disks.

Service Charge: For straightforward word processing you can charge for your time: say £4 an hour. For designing notepaper or business paper you should charge for the design and then for the amount of paper you supply: the design could be worth £5, then add the cost of the paper, plus an amount for your time, worked out per hour. But if you work *very* slowly you can't really justify charging for all your time.

Manicurist: £4.00 per manicure.

Males and females of all ages love to have their finger nails manicured. It's quite easy to do but don't attempt to cut any cuticles – you need to be trained for that! Men usually prefer not to have their nails painted.

It should be a very pleasant experience, so work gently and perhaps play some relaxing music while you work.

You Will Need

2 chairs and a table
Bowl of warm water
Towel
Tray for equipment
Hand cream
Emery boards

Cuticle stick
Cotton wool
Nail varnish (selection of colours)
Nail varnish remover

How to Give a Manicure

1. Organize all the equipment you will need laid out on a tray.
2. Sit your client comfortably on a chair facing you across a small table.
3. Soak one of his/her hands in warm water while you file the nails of the other hand with an emery board. Ask each client how they like their nails to be shaped, i.e. pointed, rounded, or straight. File towards the centre of each nail.
4. Change hands. Soak the filed hand while you dry the wet one and file its nails.
5. Massage cream into both hands. Wipe any residue off nails. Paint the nails with two coats of varnish. Use remover to clean off any smudges of varnish left around the nails.
6. Leave to dry for at least 15 minutes.

Service Charge: £4. A manicure will take about 45 minutes and you have to allow for the cost of your equipment.

Advertising and Marketing: Word of mouth, as well as make and distribute leaflets to friendly neighbours. Get in some orders *before* you spend lots of money on different colours of nail varnish.

MORE OUTDOOR SERVICES

Take my Advice!

WHERE'S THERE'S MUCK THERE'S MONEY!

Taking Out the Rubbish and Cleaning Around the Dustbins: £2.50 per month.

You Will Need
Rubber gloves,
Old clothes

Plastic bin bags for the
material to be recycled

Yes, this is a pretty yukky job but it definitely gets a *gold star* rating. Start at home by taking out the rubbish. Sort out anything that can be recycled. Once a week put out the big dustbin or black bags for collection. After the rubbish collection, put the bins away tidily and sweep around the bins. You could then leaflet other houses in the street and offer a similar rubbish service. You could charge an extra 50p–£1 for washing out a bin with hot soapy water once a month. Only offer to do this service at weekends when you have more time.

Cleaning the Car

This is one of the classic business opportunities for kids. (See page 17.)

Dog Walking Service: £3.50 a week per dog

You Will Need

Dog lead (provided by each owner)	*Ball*
	Plastic bags
Dog biscuits	*Park nearby*

Lots of people don't have time to walk their dog during the week when they have to go to work. If you're an early riser you could do this with a friend before school. Or when the evenings are light you could do it after school. Never dog walk in the park alone.

Special Skills: You must love dogs, be able to control them, and not throw-up when you *have to* pick up dog poo (with a plastic bag of course!). First, make friends with a dog in its own home. If possible, accompany the owner on a walk with the dog before you start taking it on your own. Start by taking one dog. When you're confident, you and a friend can each take two at a time.

Marketing and Advertising: Distribute flyers locally or ask if you can put up a poster at the vet's surgery or in a pet shop.

Take my Advice!

- Always dog walk with a friend.
- Try to get customers from one block of flats or from neighbouring streets so you collect all the dogs from one central point.
- Be punctual and reliable. *Most* people who need a dog walker lead very busy lives and won't want to be kept waiting.
- When the dogs are with you, they are your responsibility. Don't let them get into any trouble.
- Do not take on any dog that bites or is *not obedient*, or that is too big for you to manage.
- Make sure you have an emergency contact phone number in case anything happens.

BABY-SITTING

Reliable baby-sitters are always in demand, but don't even think about baby-sitting if you:

- can't stand small kids.
- dislike babies.
- don't want to change nappies.
- can't clear up vomit.
- don't like being *alone* in someone else's house at night.

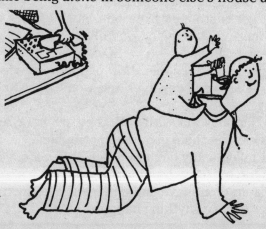

DIFFERENT BABY-SITTING SERVICES
Basic Baby-sitting: £2.50 per hour.
This is when a baby and/or young children are in bed already, their parents are going out for the evening and they need someone to be there if any of the kids wake up. You need to be at least 15 years old to baby-sit at night. Even then it is wise to share the job with a friend. The good thing about basic baby-sitting is that you are being paid while still doing what you would probably have done at home anyway, like watch TV, do your homework or read a book.

Basic Baby-sitting (+ extras): £3–£4 per hour.
If the children are still awake and you have to play with them for a while, read them a story, stay with them until they go to sleep, or change a nappy, you can charge a higher rate than for basic baby-sitting.

Tips for Baby-sitters

- If the job ends late, you should be walked or driven home, collected, or put in a taxi.
- Get an emergency contact number for the parents, *and/or* numbers to call if the parents can't be reached.
- Ask the people what you can have for a snack, or take your own grub.
- Learn some simple first-aid.
- Before they go out, ask the parents what time the children usually go to bed.
- Ask the parents what is the best way to get the child to go back to sleep.
- Do not use baby-sitting as an opportunity to use the phone. The parents may try to ring you and be angry if they can't get through. Also their telephone bill will list the time of your call and how much it cost and you could be charged for it.
- Always ask if you want to come with a friend.

Daytime Baby-sitting Service: £1.50 per hour.

This is great fun to do in the holidays and it involves keeping a baby or small child happy and entertained during the day, usually with a parent or other adult close by in case of accident or emergency. You have to be very responsible with little children. Some experience with younger brothers and sisters would be good training and worth mentioning on an advertising flyer.

How to Keep Small Children Happy

Read and look at books with them. Tell them stories. Sit and

draw with them. Blow bubbles in a bowl in the kitchen. Play dressing-up games. Play with building blocks. Dance to music. Take them to the park (preferably with another friend your own age). Play football. Make up imaginary stories about their favourite toys and dolls.

Business Opportunity: Organize a baby-sitting agency in the neighbourhood. Ask older kids if they want the work and tell them you will find it for them. They will need to be able to give you two names of people who will give them a good character reference and *you* must get in touch with those people to check if your future employees are reliable and decent. Charge the clients £3 an hour, pay the baby-sitter £2, and keep £1 for yourself for organizing the work.

Advertising and Marketing: Distribute flyers in the neighbourhood. Always try to find clients within walking or biking distance or ensure that the parents will drive you home at night.

SHOPPING SERVICE
£2 for the first bag; then 50p per bag after that.
Lots of people dislike shopping or don't have time for it.
Older people find it hard as they often do not have a car
and the bags are too heavy for them to carry.

Take my Advice!
Don't offer to buy 25 kg of potatoes and 8 litres of milk.
Your arms will drop off!

You Will Need
*A back pack (it's the easiest way to carry heavy shopping if
    you have to walk); OR*
A bicycle with panniers, back rack, or a basket.
A supermarket close to your home.
Shopping checklists

Advertising and Marketing: Produce and distribute a flyer
to likely customers. To get them to try your shopping
service, you may need to offer to do the first shopping trip
free of charge. Make it clear they only have to pay for the
goods you buy for them this once. If you do the job
efficiently you will soon have regular customers. Tell your
customers it is illegal for you to buy cigarettes or alcohol
because you are under 18. Design a shopping checklist and
always put a fresh one in the groceries when you deliver
them. Ask your customers to have the list and money to
pay for the shopping ready for you to collect in the
morning. You'll have to be careful not to lose it or have it
stolen! You can then shop on the way home from school.
Or, better still, they could ring their list through to you. In
this case, you'll have to sort out with each customer how
you are going to get the money to pay for their shopping.
  The checklist should include your name, address and
telephone number, the times you are available, and give a

general list of items to which the customer can add their own particular requirements. It will speed up your shopping if the items on the checklist are in the order that you will come to them as you walk down the aisles of your supermarket.

Gaby & Dom's SHOPPING SERVICE Phone: 123 4567	SHOPPING CHECKLIST DATE:

Available:
Weekdays after 4 p.m. Weekends between 9-11 a.m.
Fee for one bag: £2. **Additional bags**: 50p each.

Customer: ....
Address: ....
Phone number: ....

SHOPPING DAY (circle preferred day/s):

Mon.   Tue.   Wed.   Th.   Fr.   Sat.   Sun.

Amount of cash received from customer:

QUANTITY	ITEM	PRICE
	VEGETABLES: [leave space in each of these sections for customers to write in their particular requirements.] FRUIT:	
	EGGS, MEAT, FISH, CHEESE	
	TOILET ROLLS, TOOTHPASTE	
	SOAP, DETERGENT	
	BREAD, CEREALS	
	COFFEE, TEA, MILK, BUTTER	
	MAGAZINES	
	OTHER	
	TOTAL COST	
	CHANGE FOR CUSTOMER	

Garden Clearing, Bulb Planting, and Pest Control: £2–£4 per hour.

There are always opportunities for garden work. In the *autumn* there are leaves to be cleared. There are bulbs to be planted and weeds to be removed in the early *spring*. In the *summer* there are lawns to be mowed. Do some trials at home to see how long each kind of job takes. You will need to be able to give a potential client some idea of what their job is going to cost before you start. If you use your client's tools, be sure to tidy them away in the proper place when you've finished.

You Will Need

A rake	*Small garden fork*
Plastic garden bags	*Trowel*
Plastic waste bin	

Every client will know how they want a job done. Ask them for advice but always be prepared to improve on their methods to get the job done faster and more efficiently.

Planting bulbs: A cricket stump makes a perfect hole to drop a bulb in before covering it with earth. It would impress a client if you knew the little variations in how each variety of bulb should be planted (some grow best if they are planted on their side). Get a book out of the library that gives detailed instructions.

Weeding: How are you going to tell the difference between a flower and a weed? A weed can be any plant that grows where your client doesn't want it to be! Some of the more common weeds are dandelions, groundsel, chicken and couch grass. Get *very specific* instructions from your client about what *weeds* they want you to pull up.

Catching pests: You can catch lots of pests by putting out halves of fruit. A jar buried up to its rim in the ground and filled with beer dregs makes a brilliant slug trap.

Chapter Nine

APPLYING FOR JOBS
Job Application Letters

There may be times when you have to apply for a job by letter. Also, it shows great initiative if you write to someone in business to offer your services when a job has not actually been advertised. If you really want to work for someone, write to tell them about yourself and what you can do. Say you'd be interested in working for them if ever a vacancy comes up.

Points to Remember When Applying for a Job
Layout out your letter as follows:
1. Your *name, address and phone number* go in the top right hand corner.
2. *Date* on the left (about 2 lines below phone no.)
3. The name and address of the person to whom you are writing.
4. Address the person by name if you know it; otherwise start: *Dear Sir or Madam*.
5. First paragraph should give all the details of the job advertised, where you saw the ad, the date it appeared, and any reference numbers quoted in it.
6. Second and third paragraphs should say what you are doing at the moment; what skills you can offer that are *relevant* to the job; give any previous experience you have had; and say why you think you would be suitable.
7. Fourth paragraph should end by asking for an interview.
8. Sign your name and print it underneath if your handwriting is not absolutely clear. If you are enclosing anything with the letter, such as a photo, brochure or reference, write: *Enc.:* at the bottom and say what it is that you're enclosing.

The following letters are samples of the kind of letters you might need to write. Don't just copy them. Rewrite them to include only information that is relevant to you and the particular job.

YOUR NAME
Address
Phone:

8th August 1997

Mr R Smith
Bob's Disks
Box number 123
Compborough
Somewhereshire

Dear Mr Smith,

I would like to apply for the position of part-time sales assistant on Saturday mornings, as advertised in today's *Somewhereshire Post* (ref: BD/8/97).

I am in the upper fifth form at school and am currently studying for my GCSEs. I would very much like to go into the retail business when I leave school and would be glad to gain some working experience.

I feel I am particularly suited to this kind of work as I am very interested in music and have worked in a record shop during my school holidays. I am honest and reliable and good with money (I am doing GCSE Maths). As secretary of the junior members of the Compborough Tennis Club I am used to being responsible for the club funds.

I am enclosing a copy of a reference from my last part-time employer. I hope you will find my application of interest and look forward to arranging to meet you.

Yours sincerely,

Sign your name clearly

Enc.: one reference

To apply for a job that hasn't been advertised you might write something like this:

The Manager
Cyclogical Bike Shop

Dear Sir,
Although you haven't advertised for any help, I see that you sometimes employ people of about my age. I am 14.

I have had plenty of experience of repairing and maintaining bicycles. For the last four years my mother and two brothers have paid me to keep their bikes in good running order. I can repair punctures; fit new brake blocks and cables, chains, new gear hubs, and dynamo lights; and can completely strip down, clean and oil any type of bike. I have resprayed two of my own.

If ever you need a new assistant I would be very glad to hear from you.

Yours sincerely,

Good luck!

Chapter Ten

DREAMS CAN COME TRUE

Success Stories

Leo Lawson O'Neil

Leo has been in business for three years. Now just 17 years old, he's thinking of winding it up. Not because it hasn't been successful but because he's lost interest in the computer business. Also, he is determined to go to Oxford University to read Politics, Philosophy and Psychology and he needs all A-grades to get in. Leo says, "Serious business and serious studying don't go together. Besides, I want to do something interesting; just making money is BORING! I need to concentrate *all* my attention on my A-levels now."

Since he started his own company, Hedgehog Computers (now Ltd), when he was 14, Leo has made about £20,000 from his OWN BUSINESS, designing, making, selling and supplying computers. I'll repeat that! *£20,000!* Pretty impressive, eh?

Leo said, "It all happened by accident. I was given some money by my dad to buy a computer. I decided to find out all I could about them before I bought one myself and in the end thought it would be better to build my own. Which is precisely what I did. Once it was built, it wasn't quite what I wanted, so I decided to sell it *at a profit* through a secondhand [ads] magazine.

"I began by custom building computers to individual requirements, then sourced suppliers and now usually get someone else to make them for me or just buy and sell them. At first, it was the thrill, and then the money that motivated me. But now, since I have set up the business as a limited company, it's time to move on. I've learnt all I can and I want to finish my studies but I'll always do something on the side. I like having money in my pocket. Money completely changes the way you feel. Coming from the level of being a child and being told what to do, what's right and wrong, suddenly, by earning your own money, you realize that you have a voice. People will listen to you.

"But there's one very important piece of advice I would like to give to other young people who think they can make it. Running a business successfully needs a lot of hard work and determination. Also, be sure to check out all you can about the legal side. I was used by some adults and had to sell some computers at a loss because I didn't know enough about the legalities and they ripped me off, totally illegally. The key to success is commitment."

Claire Bernstein
Claire began working at 9. She was the mannequin for Marks & Spencer girl's wear.

"Between the ages of 9–11, I had to try on samples of all the clothes for girls aged 10 to see if they had been designed properly. I was going to a theatre school that acted as an agency for their students. It wasn't too hot academically, though. Anyway, I missed so much schooling during those two years through my modelling work that I left and went to another school that was more strict academically.

"It was quite boring really, trying on clothes to see if I could do up the buttons or run around in them. Because in the fashion business you always work ahead of the seasons, during the summer when it was boiling I was wrapped up in a jumper and coat, and in winter when it was freezing I would have to wear summer clothes. There was lots of hanging around. The thing that really upset me was that although they used me as a clothes mannequin because I was so gawky and thin, they used another girl who was blond with a round face to model for photography. One good thing about it was that at least I didn't have to wear my school uniform which was a disgusting yellow and green (we were known as cheesy bogies!), and the best thing was the biscuits.

"When my friends were getting pocket money each week, I would be receiving cheques. I was paid about £6 an hour, which my parents put away in a savings account for me.

"My next school only allowed us to work two days a week. I did some radio plays which was fantastic fun. Even though you are on the radio you have to actually act out the part or your voice doesn't sound authentic. Sometimes we even got to change the words in the script if we didn't understand them. I was paid about £600 for three day's work. I still get royalties, about £35 each time it's broadcast.

"My favourite job was as an extra in the television soap *Eastenders.* My mum made me wear a luminous scarf so I would stand out in the crowd. Now I have an agent but I've got a really good job that I thoroughly enjoy and I don't want to lose it through taking time off for auditions. It's very hard making a living as an actor. I would advise anyone who decides to go into the profession to take a computer course as well. That way you can always do temporary office work to earn regular money."

MAKING MONEY FOR OTHER PEOPLE

Fund-Raising for Your Favourite Charity

Now you know how to make money for yourself, you may like to know how to raise money for the charities you would most like to support.

You could simply donate to your favourite charity some of the money you earn by providing services or making and selling things. However, the *organizational, advertising* and *marketing* skills you've learned in this book will all come in handy if you want to raise even more funds for good causes. You and some friends could simply organize to collect old clothes and take them to the charity shops. Or you could use all your *networking* (page 33) and *promotion* experience to organize a sponsored event. This is one of the best ways for children to raise money for charity.

A sponsor guarantees to pay a certain amount of money to someone for taking part in an event of some kind. For example, a sponsor might pay 50p for every length you swim; or a £1 for every mile you walk, or £2 if you do the walk wearing Wellington boots filled with custard; or 10p for every day you don't eat a single sweet, or don't suck your thumb.

You will need to design a sponsorship form and ask everyone you know to sponsor you. They can choose how much or little they want to pay. Your form might look something like this:

WELLINGTON BOOT SPONSORED WALK
WITH OR WITHOUT CUSTARD!
In aid of SAVE THE CHILDREN
Registered Charity No. . . . .

On Saturday, August 10, at 11 a.m. [YOUR NAME HERE] will be walking BACKWARDS between the stumps of the Elms Avenue Cricket pitch. If you would like to sponsor him/her, please write your name and the amount per lap you would like to pay. If you make it worth his/her while (i.e. pay more!) the wellies will be squelchingly full of delicious lumpy custard. UGH!

	AMOUNT SPONSORED per cricket pitch lap		£ paid
Sponsor's Name	NO Custard	WITH Custard	
Jenny Brown	20p	£1	

The Law

Before you start to organize your sponsored event there are some legal facts you should know:

- *Before* you begin any fund-raising, you must get permission from the Charity for which you intend to raise funds.
- Every charity is registered. You must quote its name and number when you advertise an event.
- No one under 16 is legally allowed to collect sponsorship money for charity. And even then the house-to-house collections you can do must only be from relatives or friends.
- If you are raising funds regularly, open a bank account or a building society account for the money you raise. You can than arrange to pay the money over to the charity perhaps every time the account reaches a balance of £25.
- Legally, you are not allowed to approach strangers for money on behalf of a charity.
- Children are not allowed to collect money in charity 'buckets' in the street.

Don't forget all the sound business sense you've acquired. Make allowances for your expenses even when you are raising money for charity.

Below, are the names and phone numbers of some of the fund-raising offices of national and international charities that help children who may be less fortunate than you are:

Childline (national): Phone 0171 239 1000

Save the Children (international): 0171 703 5400

Oxfam (international): 0171 585 0220

Children in Need (international): 0181 992 7043

Children's Hospital, Great Ormond Street (national): 0181 944 9410

The Children's Society (national): 0171 727 1792

Childhope (international): 0171 833 0868
Comic Relief (international): 0345 460 460
Child Poverty Action Group: 0171 253 3406

There are hundreds of other charities you may want to help. Look under *Charitable Organizations* in the *Yellow Pages* to find their telephone numbers. For example, you may want to raise money for different issues, such as: homelessness (Centrepoint); human rights (Amnesty) or, women and girls' rights (Womankind); environmental protection (Friends of the Earth); old people (Age Concern); or animals (RSPCA).

If you would like more information on how charities operate visit the bookshop at:

The Directory of Social Change
The Charity Centre
24 Stephenson Way
London, NW1 2DP.
Telephone: 0171 209 0902.

Chapter Eleven

SERIOUS MONEY

Saving, Investing, and Tax

Once you begin to make money there are lots of things you can do with it. You can spend it or you can save it. Or, you can spend some of it and save some of it. The more money you save, the more money it will make for you. Money can actually be made to work for you.

If you're ever going to save money, the first basic rule is not to spend more than you earn. In other words, if you earn £1 per week do not spend £1.50. It is better to spend just 75p of it and save 25p. By the end of one month you'd have a £1 saved. And you can do a lot more with the £12 you'd have at the end of the year, than you could have by spending the single 25p each week.

Gifts of Money

Relatives, especially those who live far away, may sometimes offer to send you money instead of a present for your birthday or Christmas. Always say YES. (You know how yukky clothes presents can be; relatives never know what you like or even what would fit you.) You can always ask your close family to give you money.

Strategy

Some adults may think it a little rude for a young person to ask for money so you need to know how to put it politely and in a way that will appeal to them. How about: "I'm saving up for my future and would rather have *a little* money to put away, please." (Well, you can hardly ask for *a lot*!) Or, "I'm saving up for a new computer so I can improve my studies." (No adult can resist a swot!)

Saving and Investing

Once you have conveyed the message that you'd like the dosh rather than some ghastly lurid-pink sweater, a book on how to look after stick-insects, or another pendant on a bootlace, you can start working out what to do with your money.

Investing it in some form of savings account will make you more money because it will earn *interest*. That is, in return for investing your money to make themselves more money, your bank will pay you a small percentage of what you have saved and add it into your account. You will still be able to buy that music tape you really want or the new pair of trainers but you may have to wait a bit until your money starts to *grow*!

There are many different ways to save money, such as:

Piggy Bank or Money Box: This may save you the bother of going down to the bank and filling in forms, but you will always be tempted to break into it! It's a good idea to have two – one that is child-proof, for long-term saving; and another for short-term saving that you can get at easily whenever you need the money.

Under the bed: Perhaps not such a good idea, especially if there is a keen vacuum cleaner in the house.

The Post Office: A National Savings Investment Account can be opened with a minimum deposit of £20 and at the moment pays 4.75% *gross* interest per year if you have less than £500 in your account; and 5.25% interest on amounts over £500. *Gross* means it is paid without any tax being deducted. You need to give one month's notice (and be older than seven) before you can withdraw your cash. If you're under seven, a parent or guardian can withdraw your money on your behalf.

Banks: Many of the major banks try to encourage children to start banking with them because they believe that once you open an account you are likely to bank your money with the same bank for the rest of your life.

But beware! Although banks may tempt you with gifts of record tokens, free wallets, or cinema tickets, there are important questions you should ask before you decide which bank can look after your money. Ring or call into the local branches near you and ask for any leaflets they can give you about opening an account for a young person. Compare what each bank is offering.

For example, with Lloyds Bank you can open a *Headway* current account with just £1 if you are aged between 11–15. You can withdraw money with a cashpoint card if you're under 16 but only with the signed approval of one of your parents. The more money you have in your account, the higher the rate of interest your money will earn. For example: £250 in your account will earn 1.6% interest per year. Whereas, £500 in your account will earn 1.72%. The interest is paid into your account once a month which means after one month your £500 will have earnt about 72p interest (i.e. one twelfth of the 1.72% interest rate) and by the end of the year your account (if you haven't deposited any more money into it) would have a balance of about £508.60 (i.e. £500 plus 1.72% interest).

If you understood all that and still want to find the best place for your money, here's a guide to get you started.

1. Ask at each of the banks what kind of account is best for you. Get details and go home to study them carefully.

2. At what age does each bank allow you to open a **current account**? For example, if you are between 11–16 you can have a Barclay*Plus* account and use a cash dispenser card to withdraw your cash.

3. A **savings account** is one in which you deposit money and only occasionally draw it out. Because the money is left in the bank longer than in a current account, it can be invested by the bank to earn money. That means the bank can pay you a higher rate of interest than they do on a current account. Check which banks will let you use a cash dispenser card on a savings account.

4. Compare the interest rates paid by the different banks on savings accounts. For example, the Barclay *Plus* account pays 3.5% gross interest per year. Interest is calculated daily but credited to your account quarterly. In the long run it will be better for you to open an account with the bank that pays the highest rate of interest, than it is to get a free gift.

Building Societies: These are quite like banks but are usually for long-term saving. Once again, find out what kinds of accounts they have especially for young people and what interest rates they pay. Compare them to the banks.

If you look like having or earning *hundreds* of pounds then there are lots of other ways you can increase your money.

Adults can invest or save it on your behalf. If they open an account in your name it can earn up to £3,765 interest per year (as long as that is *all* you are *earning* each year) without any tax being deducted (see *Tax Matters*, below). Money can be invested for you in saving plans such as: Children's Bonus Bonds from National Savings; Unit Trusts; Investment Trusts; in a TESSA (tax exempt savings account) or a PEP (personal equity plan) which are operated by the banks and building societies. The Stock Market, unless you have an expert financial wizard in the family, might not be such a good idea as it can be risky. Premium Bonds have the advantage that they can be cashed in at any time.

Tax Matters
Frankly, you don't have to worry about tax unless you have huge investments or you're a highly paid film star earning thousands! When you invest money, whether it is in a savings account or in unit trusts, you, like any adult, will have to pay tax on *some* of the interest your money earns or on what you earn by working.

But read on before you throw your hands up in horror and scream, "What's the point of all those hours washing cars in arctic conditions if I don't get to keep *all* the money?"

Tax Facts (valid for 1997–98 tax year)
1. You can earn £3,765 *profit* per year *before* you have to pay any tax. This is called a *tax allowance*, that is what you're allowed to earn each year free of paying any tax. The amount you earn can be made up of interest on a bank or building society account plus any money you earn yourself. Any money you earn above this £3,765 is taxed at adult rates.
2. Your *parents* can give you a *gift* of up to £3,500 per year. You won't have to pay tax on the gift, nor does it count

as part of the £3,765 tax allowance. The gift is allowed to earn you up to £100 in interest before you have to start paying tax on the interest your money earns. Your parents will have to sign a *gross* form so the interest can be paid to into your account without first having tax deducted by the bank or building society.

If anyone else, like a grandparent or family friend, wants to give you money, they should check with their tax office what the rules are. Giving money to you, could save them from having to pay some tax.

If your folks set up a bank account for you ask them to make sure that the interest in the savings account is paid *gross*. A green form (No R85) is available for this purpose at most bank and building society branches.

Now, if you've managed to struggle through all that heady high finance without your eyelids dropping and your head clonking on to the table, I'm truly IMPRESSED. Most adults would have given up long ago and gone shopping for something they definitely couldn't afford! Afterall, if they spend, spend, spend, they won't have any money left to invest and won't have to read all those complicated leaflets to compare the interest rates. Perhaps, you could set up a business explaining to adults the finer detail of how high finance works!